GOOD TIDINGS OF GREAT JOY

A COLLECTION OF CHRISTMAS SERMONS

Charles Spurgeon

GLH Publishing
LOUISVILLE, KY

Compiled from sermons 2393, 1330, 2915, 666, 168, 57, 727, 291
   of Charles Spurgeon.

This work has been lightly edited to update include footnotes
   to aid the reader.

ISBN:

   Paperback 978-1-941129-88-3

CONTENTS

I. THE BIRTH OF CHRIST

*"Behold, a virgin shall conceive and bear a Son, and
shall call His name Immanuel. Butter and honey shall
He eat, that He may know to refuse the evil, and choose
the Good."*
Isaiah 7:14,15.

The kingdom of Judah was in a condition of imminent per-
il. Two monarchs had leagued themselves against her, two
nations had risen up for her destruction. Syria and Israel
had come up against the walls of Jerusalem with full intent
to raze them to the ground and utterly destroy the monarchy of Judah. Ahaz the king, in great trouble, exerted
all his ingenuity to defend the city and, among the other
contrivances which his wisdom taught him, he thought it
fit to cut off the waters of the upper pool, so that the be-
siegers might be in distress for lack of water. He goes out
in the morning, no doubt attended by his courtiers, makes
his way to the conduit of the upper pool, intending to see
after the stopping of the stream of water, but lo, he meets
with something which sets aside his plans and renders
them needless! Isaiah steps forward and tells him not to
be afraid for the smoke of those two firebrands, for God
should utterly destroy both the nations that had risen up
against Judah. Ahaz need not fear the present invasion, for
both he and his kingdom would be saved. The king looked
at Isaiah with an eye of incredulity, as much as to say, "If
the Lord were to send chariots from Heaven, could such a
thing as this be? Should He animate the dust and quicken
every stone in Jerusalem to resist my foes, could this be
done?"

The Lord, seeing the littleness of the king's faith,
tells him to ask for a sign. "Ask it," He says, "either in the
depth, or in the height above. Let the sun go backward
ten degrees, or let the moon stop in her midnight marches.
Let the stars move from one side to the other in the sky in
grand procession! Ask any sign you please in the Heaven

1

above, or, if you wish, choose the earth beneath, let the depths give forth the sign, let some mighty waterspout lose its way across the pathless ocean and travel through the air to Jerusalem's very gates! Let the heavens shower a golden rain instead of the watery fluid which usually they distill. Ask that the fleece may be wet upon the dry floor, or dry in the midst of dew. Whatever you please to request, the Lord will grant it to you for the confirmation of your faith." Instead of accepting this offer with all gratitude, as Ahaz should have done, he, with a pretended humility, declares that he will not ask, neither will he tempt the Lord his God! Whereupon Isaiah, waxing indignant, tells him that since he will not, in obedience to God's command, ask for a sign, behold, the Lord, Himself, will give him one—not simply a sign, but this sign, the sign and wonder of the world, the mark of God's mightiest mystery and of His most consummate wisdom, for, "a virgin shall conceive and bear a Son, and shall call His name Immanuel."

It has been said that the passage I have taken for my text is one of the most difficult in all the Word of God. It may be so—I certainly did not think it was until I saw what the commentators had to say about it and I rose up from reading them perfectly confused! One said one thing and another denied what the other had said. And if there was anything that I liked, it was so self-evident that it had been copied from one to the other and handed through the whole of them!

One set of commentators tells us that this passage refers entirely to some person who was to be born within a few months after this prophecy, "for," they say, "it says here, 'Before the child shall know to refuse the evil, and choose the good, the land that you abhor shall be forsaken of both her kings.'" "Now," say they, "this was an immediate delivery which Ahaz required and there was a promise of a speedy rescue, that, before a few years had elapsed, before the child should be able to know right from wrong, Syria and Israel should both lose their kings." Well, that seems a strange frittering away of a wonderful passage, full of meaning, and I cannot see how they can substantiate their view when we find the Evangelist Matthew quoting this very passage in reference to the birth of Christ, and saying, "Now all this was done, that it might be fulfilled which was spoken of the Lord by the Prophet, saying, Behold, a virgin shall be with Child, and shall bring forth a Son, and they shall call His name Immanuel."

It strikes me that this Immanuel, who was to be born, could not be a mere simple man and nothing else, for if you turn to the next chapter of Isaiah, at the 8th verse, you will find it said, "He [king of Assyria] shall pass through Judah; he shall overflow and go over, he shall reach even to the neck; and the stretching out of his wings shall fill the breadth of Your land, O Immanuel." Here is a government ascribed to Immanuel which could not be His if we were to suppose that the Immanuel here spoken of was either Shear-Jashub, or Maher-Shalal-Hash-Baz, or any other of the sons of Isaiah! I therefore reject that view of the matter. It is, to my mind, far below the height of this great argument—it does not speak or allow us to speak one half of the wondrous depth which couches beneath this mighty passage!

I find, moreover, that many of the commentators divide the 16th verse from the 14th and 15th verses, and they read the 14th and 15th verses exclusively of Christ, and the 16th verse of Shear-Jashub, the son of Isaiah. They say that there were two signs, one was the conception by the virgin of a Son, who was to be called Immanuel, who is none other than Christ, but the second sign was Shear-Jashub, the Prophet's son, of whom Isaiah said, "Before this child, whom I now lead before you—before this son of mine shall be able to know good and evil, so soon shall both nations that have now risen against you lose their kings." But I do not like that explanation because it seems to me to be pretty plain that the same child is spoken of in the one verse as in the others. "Before the Child"—the same Child—it does not say that Child in one verse and then this child in another verse, but before the Child, this one of whom I have spoken, the Immanuel, before He "shall know to refuse the evil, and choose the good, the land that you abhor shall be forsaken of both her kings."

Then another view, which is the most popular of all, is to refer the passage, first of all, to some child that was then to be born, and afterwards, in the highest sense, to our blessed Lord Jesus Christ. Perhaps that is the true sense of it—perhaps that is the best way of smoothing difficulties—but I think that if I had never read those books at all, but had simply come to the Bible, without knowing what any man had written upon it, I would have said, "There is Christ here as plainly as possible! Never could His name have been written more legibly than I see it here. 'Behold, a virgin shall conceive and bear a Son.' It is an unheard

of thing, it is a miraculous thing and, therefore, it must
be a God-like thing! She 'shall call His name Immanuel.
Butter and honey shall He eat, that He may know to refuse the evil, and choose the good.' And before that Child,
the Prince Immanuel, shall know to refuse the evil, and
choose the good, the land that you abhor shall be forsaken
of both her kings, and Judah shall smile upon their ruined
palaces."

This morning, then, I shall take my text as relating
to our Lord Jesus Christ, and we have three things, here,
about Him. First, the birth. Secondly, the food. And, thirdly, the name of Christ.

I. Let us commence with the birth of Christ—"Behold
a virgin shall conceive and bear a Son."

"Let us even now go unto Bethlehem and see this thing
which is come to pass," said the shepherds. "Let us follow
the star in the sky," said the Eastern Magi, and so say we
this morning. Hard by the day when we, as a nation, celebrate the birthday of Christ, let us go and stand by the
manger to behold the commencement of the Incarnation
of Jesus! Let us recall the time when God first enveloped
Himself in mortal form and tabernacled among the sons
of men! Let us not blush to go to so humble a spot—let us
stand by that village inn and let us see Jesus Christ, the
God-Man, become an Infant of a span long!

And, first, we see here, in speaking of this birth of
Christ, a miraculous conception. The text says expressly,
"Behold, a virgin shall conceive and bear a Son." This expression is unparalleled even in Sacred Writ! Of no other
woman could it be said beside the Virgin Mary, and of no
other man could it be written that his mother was a virgin.
The Greek word and the Hebrew are both very expressive
of the true and real virginity of the mother, to show us that
Jesus Christ was born of woman and not of man. We shall
not enlarge upon the thought, but still, it is an important
one, and ought not to be passed over without mentioning.
Just as the woman, by her venturous spirit, stepped first
into transgression—lest she should be despised and tram-
pled on, God, in His wisdom devised that the woman, and
the woman, alone, should be the author of the Body of the
God-Man who should redeem mankind! Albeit that she,
herself, first tasted the accursed fruit, and tempted her
husband (it may be that Adam, out of love to her, tasted
that fruit lest she should be degraded, lest she should not
stand on an equality with him), God has ordained that so

it should be, that His Son should be sent forth "born of a woman," and the first promise was that the Seed of the woman, not the seed of the man, should bruise the serpent's head.

Moreover, there was a peculiar wisdom ordaining that Jesus Christ should be the Son of the woman, and not of the man, because, had He been born of the flesh, "that which is born of the flesh is flesh," and merely flesh—and He would, naturally, by carnal generation, have inherited all the frailties and the sins and the infirmities which man has from his birth. He would have been conceived in sin and shaped in iniquity, even as the rest of us. Therefore He was not born of man, but the Holy Spirit overshadowed the Virgin Mary and Christ stands as the one Man, save one other, who came forth pure from his Maker's hands, who could ever say, "I am pure." Yes, and He could say far more than that other Adam could say concerning his purity, for He maintained His integrity and never let it go! And from His birth down to His death He knew no sin, neither was guile found in His mouth. Oh, marvelous sight! Let us stand and look at it. A Child of a virgin, what a mixture!

There is the finite and the Infinite, there is the mortal and the Immortal, corruption and Incorruption, the manhood and the Godhead, time married to eternity! There is God linked with a creature, the Infinity of the august Maker come to tabernacle on this speck of earth—the vast unbounded One whom earth could not hold and the heavens cannot contain—lying in His mother's arms! He who fastened the pillars of the universe and riveted the nails of creation, hanging on a mortal breast, depending on a creature for nourishment! Oh, marvelous birth! Oh, miraculous conception! We stand and gaze and admire. Verily, angels may wish to look into a subject too dark for us to speak of! There we leave it, a virgin has conceived and borne a Son.

In this birth, moreover, having noticed the miraculous conception, we must notice, next, the humble parentage. It does not say, "A princess shall conceive and bear a Son," but a virgin. Her virginity was her highest honor—she had no other. True, she was of royal lineage—she could reckon David among her forefathers—and Solomon among those who stood in the tree of her genealogy. She was a woman not to be despised, albeit that I speak of humble parentage, for she was of the blood-royal of Judah. O Babe, in Your veins there runs the blood of kings! The blood of an ancient monarchy found its way from Your heart all through the courses of Your body! You were born, not of mean parents, if we look at their ancient ancestry, for You are the Son of him who ruled the mightiest monarchy in his day, even Solomon, and You are the descendant of one who devised in his heart to build a Temple for the mighty God of Jacob!

Nor was Christ's mother, in point of intellect, an inferior woman. I take it that she had great strength of mind, otherwise she could not have composed so sweet a piece of poetry as that which is called the Virgin's Song, beginning, "My soul does magnify the Lord." She is not a person to be despised. I would, this morning, especially utter my thoughts on one thing which I consider to be a fault among us Protestants. Because Roman Catholics pay too much respect to the Virgin Mary, and offer prayer to her, we are too apt to speak of her in a slighting manner. She ought not to be placed under the ban of contempt, for she could truly sing, "From henceforth all generations shall call me blessed." I suppose Protestant generations are among the "all generations" who ought to call her blessed. Her name is Mary, and quaint George Herbert wrote an anagram upon it—

"How well her name an *army* does present,
Wherein whom the Lord of Hosts did pitch His tent."

Though she was not a princess, yet her name, Mary, by interpretation, signifies a princess, and though she is not the queen of Heaven, yet she has a right to be reckoned among the queens of earth. And though she is not the lady of our Lord, she does walk among the renowned and mighty women of Scripture.

Yet Jesus Christ's birth was a humble one. Strange that the Lord of Glory was not born in a palace! Princes, Christ owes you nothing! Princes, Christ is not your debtor! You did not swaddle Him, He was not wrapped in purple, you had not prepared a golden cradle for Him to be rocked in! Queens, you did not dandle Him on your knees, He hung not at your breasts! And you mighty cities, which then were great and famous, your marble halls were not blessed with His little footsteps! He came out of a village, poor and despised, even Bethlehem! When there, He was not born in the governor's house, or in the mansion of the chief man, but in a manger! Tradition tells us that His manger was cut in solid rock—there was He laid and the oxen likely enough came to feed from the same manger, the hay and the fodder of which was His only bed. Oh, wondrous stoop of condescension, that our blessed Jesus should be girded with humility and stoop so low!

Ah, if He stooped, why should He bend to such a lowly birth? And if He bowed, why should He submit, not simply to become the Son of poor parents, but to be born in so miserable a place?

Let us take courage here. If Jesus Christ was born in a manger in a rock, why should He not come and live in our rocky hearts? If He was born in a stable, why should not the stable of our souls be made into a house for Him? If He was born in poverty, may not the poor in spirit expect that He will be their Friend? If He thus endured degradation at the first, will He count it any dishonor to come to the very poorest and humblest of His creatures and tabernacle in the souls of His children? Oh, no! We can gather a lesson of comfort from His humble parentage and we can rejoice that not a queen, or an empress, but that a humble woman became the mother of the Lord of Glory!

We must make one more remark upon this birth of Christ before we pass on, and that remark shall be concerning a glorious birthday. With all the humility that surrounded the birth of Christ, there was yet very much that was glorious, very much that was honorable. No other man ever had such a birthday as Jesus Christ had! Of whom had Prophets and seers ever written as they wrote of Him? Whose name is engraved on so many tablets as His? Who had such a scroll of prophecy, all pointing to Him as Jesus Christ, the God-Man? Then remember, concerning His birth, when did God ever hang a fresh lamp in the sky to announce the birth of a Caesar? Caesars may come and they may die, but stars shall never prophesy their birth! When did angels ever stoop from Heaven and sing choral symphonies on the birth of a mighty man? No, all others are passed by, but look—in Heaven there is a great light shining and a song is heard—"Glory to God in the highest, and on earth peace, good will toward men."

Christ's birth is not despicable, even if we consider the visitors who came around His cradle. Shepherds came first and, as it has been quaintly remarked by an old Divine, the shepherds did not lose their way, but the wise men did! Shepherds came first, unguided and unfed, to Bethlehem. The wise men, directed by the star, came next. The representative men of the two bodies of mankind—the rich and

the poor—knelt around the manger—and gold, and frankincense, and myrrh, and all manner of precious gifts were
offered to the Child who was the Prince of the kings of the
earth, who, in ancient times was ordained to sit upon the
Throne of His father, David, and in the wondrous future
to rule all nations with His rod of iron!

"Behold, a virgin shall conceive and bear a Son." Thus
have we spoken of the birth of Christ.

II. The second thing that we have to speak of is the
food of Christ—"Butter and honey shall He eat, that He
may know to refuse the evil, and choose the good."

Our translators were certainly very good scholars and
God gave them much wisdom so that they craned up our
language to the majesty of the original, but here they were
guilty of very great inconsistency. I do not see how butter
and honey can make a child choose good and refuse evil.
If it is so, I am sure butter and honey ought to go up greatly in price, for good men are very much required! But it
does not say, in the original, "Butter and honey shall He
eat, that He may know to refuse the evil, and choose the
good," but, "Butter and honey shall He eat, till He shall
know how to refuse the evil, and choose the good," or,
better still, "Butter and honey shall He eat, when He shall
know how to refuse the evil, and choose the good."

We shall take that translation and just try to make clear
the meaning couched in the words. They should teach us,
first of all, Christ's proper Humanity. When He would
convince His disciples that He was flesh, and not spirit, He
took a piece of a broiled fish and of a honeycomb, and ate
as others did. "Handle Me," He said, "and see, for a spirit
has not flesh and bones, as you see I have." Some heretics
taught, even a little after the death of Christ, that His body
was a mere shadow, that He was not an actual, real Man—
but here we are told He ate butter and honey just as other
men did. While other men were nourished with food, so
was Jesus! He was very Man as certainly as He was verily
and eternally God. "In all things it behooved Him to be
made like unto His brethren, that He might be a merciful and faithful High Priest in things pertaining to God, to
make reconciliation for the sins of the people." Therefore
we are told that He ate butter and honey to teach us that it
was actually a real Man who, afterwards, died on Calvary.

The butter and honey teach us, again, that Christ was
to be born in times of peace. Such products are not to
be found in Judea in times of strife—the ravages of war

sweep away all the fair fruits of industry—the unwatered pastures yield no grass and, therefore, there could be no butter. The bees may make their hive in the lion's carcass and there may be honey there, but when the land is disturbed, who shall go to gather the sweetness? How shall the babe eat butter when its mother flees away, even in the winter time, with the child clinging to her breast? In times of war, we have no choice of food—then men eat whatever they can procure and the supply is often very scanty. Let us thank God that we live in the land of peace and let us see a mystery in this text, that Christ was born in times of peace.

The temple of Janus was shut before the Temple of Heaven was opened! Before the King of Peace came to the Temple of Jerusalem, the horrid mouth of war was stopped! Mars had sheathed his sword and all was still. Augustus Caesar was emperor of the world, none other ruled it and, therefore, wars had ceased—the earth was still, the leaves quivered not upon the trees of the field, the ocean of strife was undisturbed by a ripple, the hot winds of war blew not upon man to trouble him—all was peaceful and quiet! And then came the Prince of Peace, who, in later days, shall break the bow, cut the spear in sunder and burn the chariot in the fire.

There is another thought here. "Butter and honey shall He eat when He shall know how to refuse the evil, and choose the good." This is to teach us the precocity of Christ, by which I mean that even when He was a child, even when He lived upon butter and honey, which is the food of children, He knew the evil from the good. It is, usually, not until children leave off the food of their infancy that they can discern good from evil in the fullest sense. It requires years to ripen the faculties, to develop the judgment, to give full play to the man—in fact, to make him a man. But Christ, even while He was a Baby, even while He lived upon butter and honey, knew the evil from the good, refused the one, and chose the other. Oh, what a mighty intellect there was in that brain! While He was an Infant, surely there must have been sparklings of genius from His eyes! The fire of intellect must have often lit up that brow! He was not an ordinary Child—how would His mother talk about the wonderful things the little Prattler said! He played not as others did. He cared not to spend His time in idle amusements. His thoughts were lofty and wondrous. He understood mysteries and when He went up to the

Temple in His early days, He was not found, like the other children, playing about the courts or the markets, but sitting among the doctors, both hearing and asking them questions! His was a master-mind—"Never man spoke like this Man." So, never child thought like this Child—He was an astonishing One, the wonder and the marvel of all children, the Prince of children—the God-Man even when He was a Child! I think this is taught us in the words, "Butter and honey shall He eat when He shall know how to refuse the evil, and choose the good."

Perhaps it may seem somewhat playful, but, before I close speaking upon this part of the subject, I must say how sweet it is to my soul to believe that as Christ lived upon butter and honey, surely butter and honey drop from His lips. Sweet are His Words unto our souls, more to be desired than honey or the honeycomb! Well might He eat butter whose Words are smooth to the tried, whose utterances are like oil upon the waters of our sorrows! Well might He eat butter, who came to bind up the broken-hearted, and well did He live upon the fat of the land, who came to restore the earth to its old fertility and make all flesh soft with milk and honey, ah, honey in the heart—

  "Where can such sweetness be
   As I have tasted in Your love,
   As I have found in Thee?"

Your Words, O Christ, are like honey! I, like a bee, have flown from flower to flower to gather sweets and concoct some precious essence that shall be fragrant to me, but I have found honey drop from Your lips, I have touched Your mouth with my finger and put the honey to my lips, and my eyes have been enlightened, sweet Jesus! Every Word of Yours is precious to my soul—no honey can compare with You—well did You eat butter and honey!

And perhaps I ought not to have forgotten to say that the effect of Christ's eating butter and honey was to show us that He would not, in His lifetime, differ from other men in His outward guise. Other Prophets, when they came, were dressed in rough garments and were austere and solemn in manner. Christ came not so—He came to be a Man among men, a feaster with those that feast, an eater of honey with eaters of honey. He differed from none and, therefore, He was called a gluttonous man and a wine-bibber. Why did Christ do so? Why did He so commit Himself, as men said, though it was verily a slander? It was because

He would have His disciples not regard meats and drinks, but despise these things, and live as others do. It was because He would teach them that it is not that which goes into a man, but that which comes out, that defiles him! It is not what a man eats, with temperance, that does him injury—it is what a man says and thinks. It is not abstaining from meat, it is not the carnal ordinance of, "Touch not, taste not, handle not," that makes the fundamentals of our religion, albeit it may be good addenda thereunto. Butter and honey Christ ate, and butter and honey may His people eat! No, whatever God, in His Providence gives unto them, that is to be the food of the Child Christ.

III. Now we come to close with the name of Christ—"And shall call His name Immanuel."

I hoped, dear friends, that I would have my voice this morning, that I might talk about my Master's name. I hoped to be allowed to drive along in my swift chariot, but, as the wheels are taken off, I must be content to go as I can. We sometimes creep when we cannot go and go when we cannot run, but oh, here is a sweet name to close up with—"She shall call His name Immanuel." Others in the olden time called their children by names which had meaning in them. They did not give them the names of eminent persons whom they would very likely grow up to hate, and wish they had never heard of! They had names full of meaning which recorded some circumstance of their birth. There was Cain—"I have gotten a man from the Lord," said his mother, and she called him Cain, that is, "Gotten," or, "Acquired." There was Seth—that is, "Appointed," for his mother said, "God has appointed me another seed instead of Abel." Noah means "Rest," or, "Comfort." Ishmael was so called by his mother because God had heard her. Isaac was called, "Laughter," because he brought laughter to Abraham's home. Jacob was called the supplanter, or the crafty one, because he would supplant his brother. We might point out many similar instances—perhaps this custom was a good one among the Hebrews, though the peculiar formation of our language might not allow us to do the same, except in a certain measure.

We see, therefore, that the Virgin Mary called her son, Immanuel, that there might be a meaning in His name, "God with us." My soul, ring these words again, "God with us." Oh, it is one of the bells of Heaven! Let us strike it yet again—"God with us." Oh, it is a stray note from the sonnets of Paradise! "God with us." Oh, it is the lisping of a seraph! "God with us." Oh, it is one of the notes of the singing of Jehovah when He rejoices over His Church with singing! "God with us." Tell it, tell it, tell it—this is the name of Him who is born today—

"Hark, the herald angels sing!"

This is His name, "God with us"—God with us, by His Incarnation, for the august Creator of the world did walk upon this globe! He who made ten thousand orbs, each of them more mighty and more vast than this earth, became the Inhabitant of this tiny atom! He who was from everlasting to everlasting, came to this world of time and stood upon the narrow neck of land betwixt the two unbounded seas! "God with us." He has not lost that name—Jesus had that name on earth and He has it, now, in Heaven! He is now, "God with us."

Believer, He is God with you to protect you! You are not alone, because the Savior is with you! Put me in the desert, where vegetation grows not—I can still say, "God with us." Put me on the wild ocean and let my ship dance madly on the waves—I would still say, "Immanuel, God with us." Mount me on the sunbeam and let me fly beyond the western sea—still I would say, "God with us." Let my body dive down into the depths of the ocean and let me hide in its caverns—still I could, as a child of God say, "God with us." Yes, and in the grave, sleeping there in corruption—still I can see the footmarks of Jesus! He trod the path of all His people and His name is still, "God with us."

But if you would know this name most sweetly, you must know it by the teaching of the Holy Spirit. Has God been with us this morning? What is the use of coming to Chapel if God is not there? We might as well be at home if we have no visits of Jesus Christ and, certainly, we may come, and come, and come as regularly as that door turns on its hinges unless it is, "God with us," by the influence of the Holy Spirit! Unless the Holy Spirit takes the things of Christ and applies them to our heart, it is not, "God with us." Otherwise, God is a consuming fire. It is "God with us" that I love—

"Till God in human flesh I see,
My thoughts no comfort find."

Now ask yourselves, do you know what "God with us"

means? Has it been God with you in your tribulations, by the Holy Spirit's comforting influence? Has it been God with you in searching the Scriptures? Has the Holy Spirit shone upon the Word? Has it been God with you in conviction, bringing you to Sinai? Has it been God with you in comforting you, by bringing you, again, to Calvary? Do you know the full meaning of that name, Immanuel, "God with us"? No—he who knows it best knows little of it! Alas, he who knows it not at all is ignorant, indeed— so ignorant that his ignorance is not bliss, but will be his damnation! Oh, may God teach you the meaning of that name, Immanuel, "God with us"!

Now let us close. "Immanuel." It is wisdom's mystery, "God with us." Sages look at it and wonder. Angels desire to see it. The plumb-line of reason cannot reach half-way into its depths. The eagle wings of science cannot fly so high and the piercing eye of the vulture of research cannot see it! "God with us." It is Hell's terror! Satan trembles at the sound of it. His legions fly apace, the black-winged dragon of the Pit quails before it! Let Satan come to you suddenly and do you but whisper that word, "God with us"—back he falls—confounded and confused! Satan trembles when he hears that name, "God with us." It is the laborer's strength—how could he preach the Gospel, how could he bend his knees in prayer, how could the missionary go into foreign lands, how could the martyr stand at the stake, how could the confessor acknowledge his Master, how could men labor if that one word were taken away? "God with us," is the sufferer's comfort, is the balm of his woe, is the alleviation of his misery, is the sleep which God gives to His beloved, is their rest after exertion and toil.

Ah, and to finish, "God with us" is eternity's sonnet, is Heaven's hallelujah, is the shout of the glorified, is the song of the redeemed, is the chorus of angels, is the everlasting oratorio of the great orchestra of the sky! "God with us"—

"Hail You Immanuel, all Divine,
   In You Your Father's glories shine!
   You brightest, sweetest, fairest One,
   That eyes have seen or angels known."

Now, a happy Christmas to you all and it will be a happy Christmas if you have God with you! I shall say nothing, today, against festivities on this great birthday of

Christ. I hold that, perhaps, it is not right to have the birthday celebrated, but we will never be among those who
think it as much a duty to celebrate it the wrong way as
others the right! But we will, tomorrow, think of Christ's
birthday. We shall be obliged to do it, I am sure, however
sturdily we may hold to our rough Puritanism. And so,
"let us keep the feast, not with old leaven, neither with the
leaven of malice and wickedness; but with the unleavened
bread of sincerity and truth." Do not feast as if you wished
to keep the festival of Bacchus! Do not live, tomorrow, as if
you adored some heathen divinity. Feast, Christians, feast!
You have a right to feast. Go to the house of feasting tomorrow! Celebrate your Savior's birth. Do not be ashamed
to be glad—you have a right to be happy. Solomon says,
"Go your way, eat your bread with joy, and drink your
wine with a merry heart; for God now accepts your works.
Let your garments be always white and let your head lack
no ointment." —

  "Religion never was designed
   To make our pleasures less."

Remember that your Master ate butter and honey. Go your
way, rejoice tomorrow, but, in your feasting, think of the
Man in Bethlehem—let Him have a place in your hearts,
give Him the glory, think of the virgin who conceived
Him—but think, most of all, of the Man born, the Child
given! I finish by again saying—"A Happy Christmas To
You All!"

II. The Great Birthday

"The angel said unto them, Fear not: for, behold, I bring you good tidings of great joy, which shall be to all people."
Luke 2:10.

There is no reason upon earth, beyond that of ecclesiastical custom, why the 25th of December should be regarded as the birthday of our Lord and Savior Jesus Christ anymore than any other day from the first of January to the last day of the year. And yet some persons regard Christmas with far deeper reverence than the Lord's Day. You will often hear it asserted that, "The Bible and the Bible, alone, is the religion of Protestants," but it is not so! There are Protestants who have absorbed a great deal beside the Bible into their religion and among other things they have accepted the authority of what they call, "the Church," and by that door all sorts of superstitions have entered. There is no authority whatever, in the Word of God, for the keeping of Christmas at all! And there is certainly no reason for keeping it just now except that the most superstitious section of Christendom has made a rule that December 25th shall be observed as the birthday of the Lord and the Church, established by State Law in this land, has agreed to follow in the same track.

You are under no bondage, whatever, to regard the regulation. We owe no allegiance to the ecclesiastical powers which have made a decree on this matter, for we belong to an old-fashioned Church which does not dare to make laws, but is content to obey them. At the same time, the day is no worse than another, and if you choose to observe it and observe it unto the Lord, I doubt not that He will accept your devotion. But, if you do not observe it, but unto the Lord observe it not for fear of encouraging superstition and will-worship, I doubt not but what you shall be as accepted in the non-observance as you could have been in the observance of it!

Still, as the thoughts of a great many Christian people

will run, at this time, towards the birth of Christ—and as this cannot be wrong—I judged it meet to use ourselves of the prevailing current and float down the stream of thought. Our minds will run that way because so many around us are following customs suggestive of it. Therefore let us get what good we can out of the occasion. There can be no reason why we should not, and it may be helpful that we should, now, consider the birth of our Lord Jesus. We will do that voluntarily which we would refuse to do as a matter of obligation—we will do that simply for convenience sake which we should not think of doing because enjoined by authority or demanded by superstition!

The shepherds were keeping their flocks by night. Probably a calm, peaceful night, wherein they felt the usual difficulty of keeping their weary eyelids open as sleep demanded its due of them. All of a sudden, to their amazement, a mighty blaze lit up the heavens and turned midnight into midday! The Glory of the Lord, by which, according to the idiom of the language, is meant the greatest conceivable glory as well as a Divine Glory, surrounded and alarmed them! And in the midst of it they saw a shining spirit, a form, the like of which they had never beheld before, but of which they had heard their fathers speak, and of which they had read in the Books of the Prophets so that they knew it to be an angel.

It was, indeed, no common messenger from Heaven, but "the angel of the Lord," that choice presence angel, whose privilege it is to stand nearest the heavenly majesty, "'mid the bright ones doubly bright," and to be employed on weightiest errands from the eternal Throne of God. "The angel of the Lord came upon them." Are you astonished that at first they were afraid? Would you not be alarmed if such a thing should happen to you? The stillness of the night, the suddenness of the apparition, the extraordinary splendor of the light, the supernatural appearance of the angel—all would tend to astound them and to put them into a quiver of reverential alarm—for I doubt not there was a mixture both of reverence and of fear in that feeling which is described as being "sorely afraid."

They would have fallen on their faces to the ground in fright had there not dropped out of that, "glory of the Lord," a gentle voice, which said, "Fear not." They were calmed by that sweet comfort and enabled to listen to the announcement which followed. Then that voice, in accents sweet as the notes of a silver bell, proceeded to say, "Behold, I bring you good tidings of great joy, which shall be to all people. For unto you is born this day in the city of David a Savior, which is Christ the Lord." They were bid to shake off all thoughts of fear and to give themselves up to joy! Doubtless they did so and, among all mankind, there were none so happy at that dead of night as were these shepherds who had seen an amazing sight!

They would never forget that night and now were consulting whether they should not hasten away to gaze upon a sight which would be more delightful still, namely, the Babe of which the angel spoke! May great joy be upon us, also, while our thought shall be that the birth of Christ is the cause of supreme joy. When we have spoken upon this we shall have to enquire, to whom does that joy belong? And thirdly, we shall consider how they shall express that joy while they possess it. May the Holy Spirit now reveal the Lord Jesus to us and prepare us to rejoice in Him.

I. The birth of Christ should be the subject of supreme joy. Rightly so. We have the angelic guarantee for rejoicing because Christ is born! It is a Truth of God so full of joy that it caused the angel who came to announce it, to be filled with gladness! He had little to do with the fact, for Christ took not up angels, but He took up the seed of Abraham. But I suppose that the very thought that the Creator should be linked with the creature—that the great Invisible and Omnipotent should come into alliance with that which He, Himself, had made—caused the angel, as a creature, to feel that all creatureship was elevated and this made him glad.

Besides, there was a sweet benevolence of spirit in the angel's bosom which made him happy because he had such gladsome tidings to bring to the fallen sons of men! Although they are not our brethren, yet do angels take a loving concern in all our affairs. They rejoice over us when we repent! They are ministering spirits when we are saved and they bear us aloft when we depart! And we are sure that they can never be unwilling servants to their Lord, or tardy helpers of His beloved ones. They are friends of the Bridegroom and rejoice in His joy! They are household servants of the family of love and they wait upon us with an eager diligence which betokens the tenderness of feeling which they have towards the King's sons.

Therefore the angel delivered his message cheerfully, as became the place from which he came, the theme which brought him down and his own interest therein. He said, "I bring you good tidings of great joy," and we are sure he spoke in accents of delight. Yes, so glad were angels at this Gospel that when the discourse was over, one angel, having evangelized and given out the Gospel for the day, there suddenly appeared a band of choristers and sang an anthem loud and sweet that there might be a full service at the first propounding of the glad tidings of great joy! A multitude of the heavenly host had heard that a chosen messenger had been sent to proclaim the new-born King and, filled with holy joy and adoration, they gathered up their strength to pursue him, for they could not let him go to earth alone on such an errand!

They overtook him just as he had reached the last word of his discourse and then they broke forth in that famous chorale, the only one sung of angels that was ever heard by human ears here below, "Glory to God in the highest, and on earth peace, good will toward men." Thus, I say, they had a full service—there was Gospel ministry in rich discourse concerning Christ—and there was hearty and devout praise from a multitude all filled with heavenly joy! It was so glad a message that they could not let it be simply spoken by a solitary voice, though that were an angel's, but they must pour forth a glad chorus of praise, singing unto the Lord a new song!

Brothers and Sisters, if the birth of Jesus was so gladsome to our cousins, the angels, what should it be to us? If it made our neighbors, who had comparatively so small a share in it, sing, how should it make us leap for joy? Oh, if it brought Heaven down to earth, should not our songs go up to Heaven? If Heaven's gate of pearl was set open at its widest and a stream of shining ones came running downward to the lower skies to anticipate the time when they shall all descend in solemn pomp at the glorious advent of the great King. If it emptied Heaven for a while to make earth so glad, ought not our thoughts and praises and all our loves to go pouring up to the eternal gate, leaving earth, awhile, that we may crowd Heaven with the songs of mortal men? Yes, verily, so let it be!—

"Glory to the new born King!
Let us all the anthem sing
'Peace on earth, and mercy mild;
God and sinners reconciled.'"

For, first, the birth of Christ was the Incarnation of

God—it was God taking upon Himself human nature—a mystery, a wondrous mystery, to be believed in rather than to be defined! Yet so it was that in the manger lay an Infant who was also Infinite! A feeble Child who was also the Creator of Heaven and earth! How this could be we do not know but that it was so we assuredly believe, and therein do we rejoice! If God thus takes upon Himself human nature, then manhood is not abandoned nor given up as hopeless! When manhood had broken the bonds of the Covenant and snatched from the one reserved tree the forbidden fruit, God might have said, "I give you up, O Adam, and cast off your race. Even as I gave up Lucifer and all his host, so I abandon you to follow your own chosen course of rebellion!"

But we have now no fear that the Lord has done this, for God has espoused manhood and taken it into union with Himself! Now manhood is not put aside by the Lord as an utterly accursed thing, to be an abomination unto Him forever, for Jesus, the Well-Beloved, is born of a virgin! God would not have taken manhood into union with Himself if He had not said, "Destroy it not, for a blessing is in it." I know the curse has fallen upon men because they have sinned, but evidently not on manhood in the abstract, for else had not Christ come to take upon Himself the form of man and to be born of woman! The Word made flesh means hope for manhood, notwithstanding the Fall!

The race is not to be outlawed and marked with the brand of death and Hell, or to be utterly abandoned to destruction, for, lo, the Lord has married into the race and the Son of God has become the Son of Man! This is enough to make all that is within us sing for joy! Then, too, if God has taken manhood into union with Himself, He loves man and means man's good. Behold what manner of love God has bestowed upon us that He should espouse our nature! For God had never so united Himself with any creature before. His tender mercy had ever been over all His works, but they were still so distinct from Himself that a great gulf was fixed between the Creator and the created, so far as existence and relationship are concerned.

The Lord had made many noble intelligences, principalities and powers of whom we know little. We do not even know what those four living creatures may be who are nearest the eternal Presence—but God had never taken up the nature of any of them, nor allied Himself with them by any actual union with His Person. But, lo, He has

allied Himself with man, that creature a little lower than
the angels, that creature who is made to suffer death by
reason of his sin! God has come into union with man and,
therefore, full sure He loves him unutterably well and has
great thoughts of good towards him. If a king's son does
marry a rebel, then for that rebel race there are prospects
of reconciliation, pardon and restoration!

There must be in the great heart of the Divine One
wondrous thoughts of pity and condescending love if He
deigns to take human nature into union with Himself! Joy,
joy forever! Let us sound the fond cymbals of delight for
the Incarnation bodes good to our race! If God has taken
manhood into union with Himself, then God will feel for
man! He will have pity upon him! He will remember that
he is dust. He will have compassion upon his infirmities
and sicknesses. You know, Beloved, how graciously it is
so, for that same Jesus who was born of a woman at Bethlehem is touched with the feelings of our infirmities, having been tempted in all points like we are! Such intimate
practical sympathy would not have belonged to our great
High Priest if He had not become Man!

Not even though He is Divine could He have been
perfect in sympathy with us if He had not, also, become
bone of our bone and flesh of our flesh. The Captain of our
salvation could only be made perfect through suffering—it
is necessary that since the children were partakers of flesh
and blood, He, Himself, also should take part of the same.
For this, again, we may ring the silver bells, since the Son
of God now intimately sympathizes with man because He
is made in all points like unto His brethren!

Further, it is clear that if God condescends to be so intimately allied with manhood, He intends to deliver man
and to bless him. Incarnation prophesies salvation. Oh, believing Soul, your God cannot mean to curse you! Look at
God Incarnate! What do you see there but salvation? God
in human flesh must mean that God intends to set man
above all the works of His hands and to give him dominion, according to His first intent, over all sheep and oxen
and all that pass through the paths of the sea and the air!
Yes, it must mean that there is to be a man beneath whose
feet all things shall be placed, so that even Death, itself,
shall be subject unto Him. When God stoops down to man
it must mean that man is to be lifted up to God! What joy
there is in this! Oh that our hearts were but half alive to the
Incarnation! Oh that we did but know a thousandth part

of the unutterable delight which is hidden in this thought, that the Son of God was born a Man at Bethlehem! Thus you see that there is overflowing cause for joy in the birth of Christ because it was the Incarnation of the Deity.

But further, the angel explained our cause for joy by saying that He, who was born, was unto us a Savior. "Unto you is born this day a Savior." Brothers and Sisters, I know who will be most glad, today, to think that Christ was born a Savior. It will be those who are most conscious of their sinnership! If you would draw music out of that ten-stringed harp—the word, "Savior"—pass it over to a sinner. "Savior" is the harp, but "sinner" is the finger that must touch the strings and bring forth the melody. If you know yourself lost by nature and lost by practice. If you feel sin like a plague at your heart. If evil wearies and worries you. If you have known the burden and the shame of iniquity, then will it be bliss to you even to hear of that Savior whom the Lord has provided!

Even as a Babe, Jesus, the Savior, will be precious to you! But most of all because He has now finished all the work of your salvation! You will look to the commencement of that work and then survey it even to its close and bless and magnify the name of the Lord. Unto you, O you who are the chief of sinners, even unto you, you consciously guilty ones, is born a Savior! He is a Savior by birth—for this purpose is He born! To save sinners is His birthright and office! It is from now on an institution of the Divine dominion and an office of the Divine Nature to save the lost! Henceforth God has laid help upon One that is mighty, and exalted One chosen out of the people, that He may seek and save that which was lost. Is there not joy in this? Where else is joy if not here?

Next, the angel tells us that this Savior is Christ the Lord and there is much gladness in that fact. "Christ," signified anointed. Now when we know that the Lord Jesus Christ came to save, it is most pleasant to perceive, in addition, that the Father does not let Him enter upon His mission without the necessary qualifications. He is anointed of the Highest that He may carry out the offices which He has undertaken—the Spirit of the Lord rested upon Him without measure! Our Lord is anointed in a threefold sense, as Prophet, Priest and King. It has been well observed that this anointing, in its threefold power, never rested upon any other man. There have been kingly prophets, David to wit. There was one kingly priest, even

Melchisedec. And there have also been priestly Prophets
such as Samuel. Thus it has come to pass that two of the
offices have been united in one man, but the whole three—
Prophet, Priest and King—never met in one thrice-anoint-
ed being until Jesus came. We have the fullest anointing
conceivable in Christ, who is anointed with the oil of gladness above His fellows. And as the Messiah, the Sent One
of God, Jesus Christ is completely prepared and qualified
for all the work of our salvation. Let our hearts be glad! We
have not a nominal Savior, but a Savior fully equipped! He
is One who in all points is like ourselves, for He is Man,
but in all points fit to help the feebleness which He has
espoused, for He is the anointed Man.

See what an intimate mingling of the Divine and human is found in the angel's song. They sing of Him as "a
Savior," and a Savior must of necessity be Divine in order
to save from death and Hell. And yet the title is drawn
from His dealings with humanity! Then they sing of Him
as, "Christ," and that must be human, for only man can
be anointed, yet that unction comes from the Godhead!
Sound forth the jubilee trumpets for this marvelously
Anointed One and rejoice in Him who is your Priest, to
cleanse you, your Prophet to instruct you and your King
to deliver you! The angels sang of Him as Lord, and yet
as born. So here, again, the godlike in dominion is joined
with the human in birth. How well did the words and the
sense agree!

The angel further went on to give these shepherds
cause for joy by telling them that while their Savior was
born to be the Lord, yet He was so born in lowliness that
they would find Him a Babe, wrapped in swaddling cloths,
lying in a manger. Is there cause of joy there? I say, yes,
indeed, there is, for it is the terror of the Godhead which
keeps the sinner, oftentimes, away from reconciliation!
But see how the Godhead has graciously concealed itself
in a Babe, a little Babe—a Babe that needed to be wrapped
in swaddling bands like any other new-born child! Who
fears to approach Him? Who ever heard of trembling in
the presence of a babe? Yet is the Godhead there!

My soul, when you cannot, for very amazement,
stand on the sea of glass mingled with fire. When the Divine Glory is like a consuming fire to your spirit and the
sacred majesty of Heaven is altogether overpowering to
you, then come to this Babe, and say, "Yet God is here,
and here can I meet Him in the Person of His dear Son,

in whom dwells all the fullness of the Godhead bodily."
Oh, what bliss there is in Incarnation if we remember that
herein God's Omnipotence comes down to man's feebleness and infinite Majesty stoops to man's infirmity! Now
mark, the shepherds were not to find this Babe wrapped
in Tyrian purple nor swathed in choicest fabrics fetched
from afar—

> "No crown bedecks his forehead fair,
>   No pearl, nor gem, nor silk is there."

Nor would they discover Him in the marble halls of princes, nor guarded by praetorian legionaries, nor pampered
by vassal sovereigns. They would find Him the Babe of a
peasant woman, of princely lineage it is true, but of a family whose stock was dry and forgotten in Israel. The Child
was reputed to be the son of a carpenter. If you looked on
the humble father and mother and at the poor bed they
had made up, where earlier oxen had come to feed, you
would say, "This is condescension, indeed."

O you poor, be glad, for Jesus is born in poverty and
cradled in a manger! O you sons of toil, rejoice, for the
Savior is born of a lowly virgin and a carpenter is His fos-
ter father. O you people, oftentimes despised and downtrodden, the Prince of the Democracy is born—one chosen
out of the people is exalted to the throne! O you who call
yourselves the aristocracy, behold the Prince of the kings
of the earth, whose lineage is Divine and yet there is no
room for Him in the inn! Behold, O men, the Son of God,
who is bone of your bone, intimate with all your griefs!
Who in His life was hungry as you are hungry, was weary as you are weary and wore humble garments like your
own! Yes, He suffered worse poverty than you, for He was
without a place where to lay His head! Let the heavens
and the earth be glad since God has so fully, so truly, come
down to man!

Nor is this all. The angel called for joy, and I ask for it,
too, on this ground, that the birth of this child was to bring
Glory to God in the highest, on earth peace, good will toward men. The birth of Christ has given such Glory to God
as I know not that He could ever have had here by any
other means! We must always speak in accents soft and
low when we talk of God's Glory. In itself it must always
be infinite and not to be conceived by us. And yet may we
not venture to say that all the works of God's hands do
not glorify Him so much as the gift of His dear Son—that

all creation and all Providence do not so well display the
heart of Deity as when He gives His Only-Begotten and
sends Him into the world that men may live through Him?
What wisdom is manifested in the plan of redemption of
which the Incarnate God is the center! What love is there
revealed! What power is that which brought the Divine
One down from glory to a manger? Only Omnipotence
could have worked so great a marvel! What faithfulness to
ancient promises! What truthfulness in keeping covenant!
What grace, and yet what justice! For it was in the Person
of that newborn Child that the Law must be fulfilled and
in His precious body must vengeance find recompense for
injuries done to Divine righteousness! All the attributes of
God were in that little Child most marvelously displayed
and veiled. Conceive the whole sun to be focused to a
single point and yet so softly revealed as to be endurable
by the most tender eyes—even thus the glorious God is
brought down for man to see Him born of a woman!

Think of it! The express image of God in mortal flesh!
The heir of all things cradled in a manger! Marvelous is
this! Glory to God in the highest! He has never revealed
Himself before as He now manifests Himself in Jesus!

It is through our Lord Jesus being born that there is
already a measure of peace on earth and boundless peace
yet to come. Already the teeth of war have been somewhat
broken and a testimony is borne by the faithful against
this great crime. The religion of Christ holds up its shield
over the oppressed and declares tyranny and cruelty to be
loathsome before God. Whatever abuse and scorn may be
heaped upon Christ's true minister, he will never be silent
while there are downtrodden nationalities and races needing his advocacy. Nor will God's servants anywhere, if
faithful to the Prince of Peace, ever cease to maintain peace
among men to the utmost of their power. The day comes
when this growing testimony shall prevail and nations
shall learn war no more. The Prince of Peace shall snap
the spear of war across His knee. He, the Lord of all, shall
break the arrows of the bow, the sword and the shield and
the battle—and He shall do it in His own dwelling place,
even in Zion, which is more glorious and excellent than
all the mountains of prey! As surely as Christ was born at
Bethlehem, He will yet make all men brothers and estab-
lish a universal monarchy of peace, of which there shall
be no end. So let us sing if we value the Glory of God, for
the new-born Child reveals it! And let us sing if we value

peace on earth, for He is come to bring it! Yes, and if we love the link which binds glorified Heaven with pacified earth—the good will towards men which the Eternal herein manifests—let us give a third note to our hallelujah and bless and magnify Immanuel, God with us, who has accomplished all this by His birth among us. "Glory to God in the highest, and on earth peace, good will toward men."

I think I have shown you that there was room enough for joy for the shepherds, but you and I, who live in later days, when we understand the whole business of salvation, ought to be even more glad than they were, though they glorified and praised God for all the things that they had heard and seen. Come, my brothers and sisters, let us at least do as much as these simple shepherds and exult with our whole souls!

II. Secondly, let us consider to whom this joy belongs. I was very heavy yesterday in spirit, for this dreary weather tends greatly to depress the mind—

"No lark could pipe to skies so dull and gray."

But a thought struck me and filled me with intense joy. I tell it to you, not because it will seem anything to you, but as having gladdened myself. It is a bit all for myself to be placed in a parenthesis! It is this, that the joy of the birth of Christ in part belongs to those who tell of it, for the angels who proclaimed it were exceedingly glad, as glad as glad could be! I thought of this and whispered to my heart, "As I shall tell of Jesus born on earth for men, I will take license to be glad, also, glad if for nothing else that I have such a message to bring to them." The tears stood in my eyes and stand there even now, to think that I should be privileged to say to my fellow men, "God has condescended to assume your nature that He might save you." These are as glad and as grand words as he of the golden mouth could have spoken. As for Cicero and Demosthenes, those eloquent orators had no such theme to dwell upon! Oh, joy, joy, joy! There was born into this world a Man who is also God! My heart dances as David danced before the Ark of God!

This joy was meant, not for the tellers of the news alone, but for all who heard it. The glad tidings "shall be unto all people." Read, "all the people," if you like, for so, perhaps, the letter of the original might demand. Well, then, it meant that it was joy to all the nation of the Jews— but assuredly our version is truer to the inner spirit of the

text—it is joy to all people upon the face of the earth that
Christ is born! There is not a nation under Heaven but
what has a right to be glad because God has come down
among men! Sing together, you waste places of Jerusalem!
Take up the strain, O you dwellers in the wilderness, and
let the multitude of the isles be glad! You, who beneath the
frigid zone, feel in your very marrow all the force of God's
north wind, let your hearts burn within you at this happy
truth! And you whose faces are scorched by the heat of the
torrid sun, let this be as a well of water unto you! Exult and
magnify Jehovah that His Son, His Only-Begotten, is also
Brother to mankind!—

> "O wake our hearts, in gladness sing!
> And hail each one the newborn King,
> Till living song from loving souls
> Like sound of mighty waters rolls."

But, Brothers and Sisters, they do not all rejoice, not
even all of those who know this glorious Truth of God. Nor
does it stir the hearts of half of mankind. To whom, then, is
it a joy? I answer, to all who believe it and especially to all
who believe it as the shepherds did—with that faith which
staggers not through unbelief. The shepherds never had
a doubt! The light, the angels and the song were enough
for them. They accepted the glad tidings without a single
question. In this the shepherds were both happy and wise,
yes, wiser than the would-be wise whose wisdom can only
manifest itself in quibbling. This present age despises the
simplicity of a childlike faith, but how wonderfully God is
rebuking its self-conceit. He is taking the wise in their own
craftiness. I could not but notice in the late discovery of
the famous Greek cities and the sepulchers of the heroes,
the powerful rebuke which the spirit of skepticism has
received! These wise doubters have been taken on their
own ground and put to confusion! Of course they told us
that old Homer was, himself, a myth, and the poem called
by his name was a mere collection of unfounded legends
and mere tales. Some ancient songster did but weave his
dreams into poetry and foist them upon us as the blind
minstrel's song—there was no fact in it, they said, nor,
indeed, in any current history—everything was mere leg-
end. Long ago these gentlemen told us that there was no
King Arthur, no William Tell, no anybody indeed! Even as
they questioned all sacred records, so have they cast sus-
picion upon all else that common men believe. But lo, the

ancient cities speak! The heroes are found in their tombs! The child's faith is vindicated! They have disinterred the king of men and this and other matters speak in tones of thunder to the unbelieving ear, and say, "You fools! The simpletons believed and were wiser than your 'culture' made you. Your endless doubts have led you into false-hood and not into truth."

The shepherds believed and were glad as glad could be, but if Professor—(never mind his name) had been there on that memorable night, he would certainly have debated with the angel and denied that a Savior was needed at all! He would coolly have taken notes for a lecture upon the nature of light and have commenced a disquisition upon the cause of certain remarkable nocturnal phenomena which had been seen in the fields near Bethlehem. Above all, he would have assured the shepherds of the absolute non-existence of anything superhuman! Have not the learned men of our age proved that impossibility, scores of times, with sufficient arguments to convince a wooden post? They have made it as plain as that three times two are eighteen that there is no God, nor angel, nor spirit! They have proven beyond all doubt, as far as their own dogma-tism is concerned, that everything is to be doubted which is most sure and that nothing is to be believed at all except the infallibility of pretenders to science. But these men find no comfort. Neither are they so weak as to need any, so they say. Their teaching is not glad tidings but a wretched negation, a killing frost which nips all noble hopes in the bud and in the name of reason steals away from man his truest bliss! Be it ours to be as philosophical as the shep-herds, for they did not believe too much, but simply be-lieved what was well attested—and this they found to be true upon personal investigation. In faith lies joy. If our faith can realize, we shall be happy. I want, this morning, to feel as if I saw the Glory of the Lord still shining in the heavens, for it was there, though I did not see it. I wish I could see that angel, and hear him speak, but, failing this, I know he did speak, though I did not hear him. I am cer-tain that those shepherds told no lies, nor did the Holy Spirit deceive us when He bade His servant, Luke, write this record! Let us forget the long interval between and only remember that it was really so. Realize that which was, indeed, matter of fact, and you may almost hear the angelic choir up in yonder sky still singing, "Glory to God in the highest, and on earth peace, good will toward men."

At any rate, our hearts rehearse the anthem and we feel the joy of it by simply believing, even as the shepherds did.

Mark well that believing what they did, these simple-minded shepherds desired to approach nearer the marvelous Babe. What did they do but consult together and say, "Let us now go to Bethlehem and see this thing which has come to pass"? O Beloved, if you want to get the joy of Christ, come near to Him! Whatever you hear about Him from His own Book, believe it! But then say, "I will go and find Him." When you hear the voice of the Lord from Sinai, draw not near unto the flaming mountain—the Law condemns you, the Justice of God overwhelms you. Bow at a humble distance and adore with solemn awe. But when you hear of God in Christ, hasten there! Hasten there with all confidence, for you are not come unto the mountain that might not be touched, and that burned with fire—you are come unto the blood of sprinkling, which speaks better things than that of Abel! Come near, come nearer, nearer still! "Come," is His own word to those who labor and are heavy laden, and that same word He will address to you at the last—"Come, you blessed of My Father, inherit the kingdom prepared for you from before the foundation of the world." If you want joy in Christ, come and find it in His bosom, or at His feet! There John and Mary found it long ago.

And then, my brethren, do what the shepherds did when they came near. They rejoiced to see the Babe of whom they had been told! You cannot see with the physical eye, but you must meditate—and so see with the mental eyes this great, grand and glorious truth that the Word was made flesh and dwelt among us! This is the way to have joy today, joy such as fitly descends from Heaven with the descent of Heaven's King! Believe! Draw near! And then fixedly gaze upon Him and so be blest.

> "Hark how all the vault of Heaven rings
>   Glory to the King of kings!
>   Peace on earth and mercy mild,
>   God and sinners reconciled.
>
> "Veiled in flesh the Godhead see;
>   Hail the incarnate Deity,
>   Pleased as Man with men to appear,
>   Jesus our Immanuel here."

III. My time has fled, else I desired to have shown, in

the third place, how that joy should be manifested. I will only give a hint or two. The way in which many believers in Christmas keep the feast we know too well. This is a Christian country, is it not? I have been told so, so often, that I suppose it must be true. It is a Christian country! But the Christianity is of a remarkable kind! It is not only that in the olden times, "Christmas broached the mightiest ale," but nowadays Christmas keepers must get drunk upon it! I slander not our countrymen when I say that drunkenness seems to be one of the principal items of their Christmastide delight. If Bacchus were born at this time, I do think England keeps the birthday of that detestable deity most appropriately, but tell me not that it is the birth of the holy Child Jesus that they thus celebrate! Is He not crucified afresh by such blasphemy? Surely to the wicked, Jesus says, "What have you to do to keep my birthday and mention my name in connection with your gluttony and drunkenness?" Shame that there should be any cause for such words! Tenfold shame that there should be so much!

You may keep His birthday all the year round, for it were better to say He was born every day of the year than on any one, for truly in a spiritual sense He is born every day of every year in some men's hearts! And that, to us, is a far weightier point than the observation of holy days! Express your joy, first, as the angels did, by public ministry. Some of us are called to speak to the many. Let us, in the clearest and most earnest tones proclaim the Savior and His power to rescue man. Others of you cannot preach, but you can sing. Sing, then, your anthems and praise God with all your hearts! Do not be slack in the devout use of your tongues, which are the glory of your frames, but again and again and again lift up your joyful hymns unto the new-born King! Others of you can neither preach nor sing. Well, then, you must do what the shepherds did, and what did they do? You are told twice that they spread the news. As soon as they had seen the Babe, they made known abroad the saying that was told them, and as they went home they glorified God. This is one of the most practical ways of showing your joy. Holy conversation is as acceptable as sermons and anthems. There was also one who said little, but thought the more—"Mary pondered all these things in her heart." Quiet, happy spirit, weigh in your heart the grand truth that Jesus was born at Bethlehem. Immanuel, God with us—weigh it if you can! Look at it again and again! Examine the varied facets of this

priceless brilliant diamond and bless, and adore and love
and wonder, and yet adore again this matchless miracle
of love!

Lastly, go and do good to others. Like the wise men,
bring your offerings and offer to the newborn King your
heart's best gold of love, frankincense of praise and myrrh
of penitence. Bring everything of your heart's best and
something of your substance, also, for this is a day of good
tidings and it were unseemly to appear before the Lord
empty. Come and worship God manifest in the flesh and
be filled with His light and sweetness by the power of the
Holy Spirit. Amen.

III. A VISIT TO BETHLEHEM

"Let us now go to Bethlehem and see this thing which is come to pass, which the Lord has made known unto us."
Luke 2:15.

Not to Bethlehem as it now is, but to Bethlehem as it once was, I would lead your meditation this evening. Were you to visit the site of that ancient city of Judah as it is at present, you would find little enough to edify your hearts. About six miles south of Jerusalem, on the slope of a hill, lies a small, irregular village, never at any time considerable either in its extent or because of the wealth of its inhabitants. The only building worthy of notice is a convent. Should your fancy paint, as you approach it, a courtyard, a stable, or a manger, you would be sorely disappointed on your arrival! Tawdry decorations are all that would greet your eyes—rather adapted to obliterate than to preserve the sacred interest with which a Christian would regard the place. You might walk upon the marble floor of a chapel and gaze on walls bedecked with pictures and studded with the fantastic dolls and other nicknacks which are usually found in Roman Catholic places of worship. Within a small grotto you might observe the exact spot that superstition has assigned to the nativity of our Lord. There a star, composed of silver and precious stones, surrounded by golden lamps, might remind you, but merely as a parody, of the simple story of the Evangelists. Truly, Bethlehem was always little, if not the least, among the thousands of Judah—and only famous for its historic associations.

So, Beloved, "let us now go to Bethlehem" as it was—let us, if possible, bring the wondrous story of that "Child born," that "Son given," down to our own times. Imagine the event to be occurring just now. I will try to paint the picture for you with vivid colors, that you may apprehend afresh the great truth of God and be impressed, as you ought to be, with the facts concerning the birth of our Lord and Savior Jesus Christ.

I propose now to make a visit to Bethlehem and I need five companions to render the visit instructive. So I would have, first, an aged Jew. Next, an ancient Gentile. Then, a convicted sinner. Next, a young believer And, last of all, an advanced Christian. Their remarks can scarcely fail to please and profit us. Afterwards I should like to take a whole family to the manger, let them all look at the divine Infant and hear what each one has to say about Him.

I. To begin, then, i would go to Bethlehem with an aged Jew.

Come on, my venerable, long-bearded brother—you are an Israelite, indeed, for your name is Simeon. Do you see the Baby "wrapped in swaddling clothes, lying in a manger"? Yes, he does and, overpowered by the sight, he clasps the Child in his arms and exclaims, "Lord, now let Your servant depart in peace, according to Your Word: for my eyes have seen Your salvation." "Here," says this faithful son of Abraham, "is the fulfillment of a thousand prophecies and promises! The hope, the expectation and the joy of my noble ancestry! Here is the Antitype of all those mystic symbols and typical offerings enjoined in the Laws of Moses. You, O Son of the Highest, are Abraham's promised Seed, the Shiloh whose coming Jacob foretold, great David's greater Son and Israel's rightful King! Our Prophets did herald your coming in each prophetic page. Our bards vied with one another who should chant Your praise in sweetest stanzas! And now, O happy hour— these poor dim eyes do greet Your beauteous form! It is enough—and more than enough—O God! I ask not that I may live any longer on earth!" So speaks the aged Jew and, as he speaks, I mark the rapturous smile that lights up every feature of his face and listen to the deep, mellow tones of his tremulous voice. As he gazes on the tender Baby, I hear him quote Isaiah's words, "He shall grow up before Him as a tender plant" and then, as he glances aside at the virgin-mother, descendant of the royal house of David, he quickly looks back to the sinless Baby and says, "A root out of a dry ground." Farewell, venerable Jew, your talk sounds sweet in my ears—may the day soon dawn when all your brethren shall return to their fatherland and there confess our Jesus as their Messiah and their King!

II. My next companion shall be an ancient Gentile.

He is an intelligent man. Do not ask me any questions concerning his creed. Deeply versed in the works of God in nature, he has glimmering, flickering light of God enough to detect the moral darkness by which he is surrounded, albeit the truth of the Gospel has not yet found an entrance into his heart. Call him a skeptic, from the heathen point of view, if you please, but his is not a willful perversion of the heart, it is rather that transition state of the mind wherein false hopes are rejected, but the true hope has not yet been espoused. This Gentile is staying at Jerusalem and we walk and talk together as we bend our steps toward Bethlehem. He has told me what pleasure he feels in reading the Jewish Scriptures and how he has often longed for the dawn of that day which their seers predict. Now we enter the house—a star shines brightly in the sky and hovers over the stable—we look at the Child and my comrade exclaims in ecstasy, "a Light to lighten the Gentiles!" "Fair Child of promise," he says, "Your birth shall be a joy to all people! Prince of Peace, Yours shall be a peaceful reign! Kings shall bring presents to You; all nations shall serve You. The poor shall rejoice in Your advent, for justice shall be done to them by You. And oppressors shall tremble at Your coming, for judgment upon them shall be pronounced by Your lips." Then sweetly did he speak of the hopes which had bloomed in that birth-chamber. He looked as if, in that same hour, he saw the application of many an ancient promise with the letter of which he was already acquainted, to the wonderful Child he there saw. It was refreshing to hear that entire quote from the evangelical Prophet, words like these, "The wolf also shall dwell with the lamb and the leopard shall lie down with the kid; and the calf and the young lion and the fatling together; and a little child shall lead them."

As I bid adieu to this friend, you must allow me to offer you one or two of my own reflections. When God, in His anger, hid His face from the house of Jacob, He lifted up the light of His countenance on the Gentiles. When the fruitful land became a desert, the wilderness, at the same time, began to blossom as the garden of the Lord. Moses had anticipated both of these events and the inspired Prophets had foreseen one as much as the other. The heart of the Jewish people made gross, the heaviness of their eyes and the dullness of their ears are not more striking as an exact fulfillment of Divine Judgment, than the extreme susceptibility of the Gentile mind to receive the evidence of our Lord's Messiahship and to embrace His Gospel! Thus had Jehovah said, fifteen hundred years before, "I will move them to jealousy with those which are not a people. I will provoke them to anger with a foolish nation." Marvel not, then, but admire the crisis in history when Paul and Barnabas were commissioned to say to the Jews who rejected the Gospel, "Lo, we turn to the Gentiles." I have consulted the map and looked with intense emotion at the route which Paul and Barnabas took on their first missionary journey. Antioch, the city from which they went forth, is situated directly North of Jerusalem—and there, in not very unequal proportions, they could find both Jews and Gentiles. "To the Jew first," was according to the divine injunction and, on their own nation rejecting the grace of God, lo, they turned to the Gentiles with a result immediately following that greatly cheered them, for the Gentiles heard with gladness and glorified the Word of the Lord! As you follow the various journeys of the Apostle Paul, you will see that his course was ever Northward, or, rather, in a North-Westerly direction—and so the tidings of the Gospel traveled on until the Church of the Redeemed found a central point in our highly-favored island! I think I hear some of you say, "We are not antiquarian enough to appreciate the society of your two venerable companions." Well then, beloved, the three that follow shall be drawn from among yourselves—and it may be that you will discover your own thoughts expressed in the sketches I am about to add.

III. Next in order is the awakened sinner.

Come here, my sister, I am glad to see you and I shall have much pleasure in your company to Bethlehem. Why do you start back? Do not be afraid! There is nothing to terrify you here. Come in! Come in! With trembling apprehension my sister advances to the rough crib where the young Child lies. She looks as if she feared to rejoice and is beyond measure astonished at herself that she does not faint. She says to me, "And is this, Sir, really and truly the great mystery of godliness? Do I, in that manger, behold 'God manifest in the flesh'? I expected to see something very different." Looking into her face, I clearly perceived that she could scarcely believe for joy. A humble, but not uninteresting visitor to the birthplace of my Lord is this trembling penitent. I wish I could have many like her out of this congregation tonight. You would see how mystery is dissolved in mercy! No flaming sword turning every way obstructs your entrance. No ticket of admission is demanded by a surly menial at the door. No favor is shown to rank or title—you may go freely in to see the noblest

Child of woman born in the humblest cot wherein infants ever nestled! Nor does a visible tiara of light encircle His brow. Too humble, I assure you, for the fancy of the poet to describe, or the pencil of the artist to sketch—like a poor man's child, he is wrapped in swaddling clothes and cradled in a manger. It needs faith to believe what the eyes of sense never could discern as you look upon "the Prince of Life" in such humble guise!

IV. My fourth companion is a young believer.

Well, my brother, you and I have often had sweet communion together concerning the things of the Kingdom. "Let us now go to Bethlehem and see this thing which is come to pass, which the Lord has made known unto us." I mark the sacred cheerfulness of my young friend's countenance as he approaches the Incarnate Mystery! Often have I heard him discussing curious doctrinal subtleties, but now, with calmness of spirit, he looks on the face of the divine Child and says, "Truth is sprung out of the earth, for a woman has brought forth her Son and righteousness has looked down from Heaven, for God has, of a truth, revealed Himself in that Baby." He looks so wistfully at the young Child, as if a fresh spring of holy gratitude had been opened in his heart. "No vision, no imagination, no myth here," he says, "but a real partaker of our flesh and blood! He has not taken on Him the nature of angels, but the seed of Abraham. Heaven and earth have united to make us blessed. Might and weakness have joined hands here!" He pauses to worship, then speaks again, "In what a small, weak, slender tabernacle do You, O glorious God, now deign to dwell! Surely, mercy and truth have here met together, righteousness and peace have kissed each other! O Jesus, Savior, You are mercy itself—the tender mercy of our God is embodied in You. You are the Truth— the very truth which the Prophets longed to see and into which the angels desire to look—the truth my soul so long sought for, but never found till I beheld Your face. Once I thought that the truth was hidden in some profound treatise, or in some learned book, but now I know that it is revealed in You, O Jesus, my Kinsman, yet Your Father's equal! And, sweet Baby, You are also righteousness—the only righteousness that God can accept. What condescension, yet what patience! Ah, dear Child, how still You lie! I wonder that, conscious of your divine power, you can thus endure the weary, lingering hours of Infancy with humility so strange, so rare! I think if you had stood by me

and watched over me in my infant weakness, that would
have been a service that I could well admire, but 'tis past
imagination's utmost stretch to realize what it must be for
you to be thus feeble, thus helpless, thus needing to be fed
and waited upon by an earthly mother! For the wonderful,
the mighty God to stoop thus, is humility profound!"

So spoke the young believer and I liked his speech
very much, for I saw in him how faith could work by love
and how the end of controversy and argument is reached
at Bethlehem, for "without controversy great is the mystery of godliness: God was manifest in the flesh."

V. Now I will go to Bethlehem with an advanced
Christian, such an one as Paul the Aged, or John the Divine—no, rather with such an one as I might find among
the circle of my own Church members!

Calm, peaceful, kind and gracious, he seems as if his
training in the school of Christ and the sacred anointing
of the Holy Spirit have made him like a child, himself—
his character is ripening and his fitness for the Kingdom
of Heaven is becoming more apparent. Tears glistened in
the old man's eyes as he looked with expressive fondness
on that "Infant of Eternal Days." He spoke not much and
what he said was not exactly like what any of my other
companions had spoken. It was his manner to quote short
sentences, with great exactness, from the Word of God.
He uttered them slowly, pondered them deeply and there
was much spiritual unction in the accent with which he
spoke. I will just mention a few of the profitable sentences
that he uttered. First he said, "No man has ascended up to
Heaven, but He that came down from Heaven, even the
Son of Man which is in Heaven." He really appeared to
see more in that passage than I had ever seen there. Jesus,
the Son of Man, in Heaven even while He was on earth!
Then he looked at the Child and said, "The same was in
the beginning with God." After that, he uttered these three
short sentences in succession, "In the beginning was the
Word—"all things were made by Him"—"and the Word
was made flesh." He looked as if he realized what a great
mystery it was that our Lord Jesus first made all things
and afterwards was Himself "made flesh." Then he reverently bent his knee, clasped his hands and exclaimed, "My
Father's gift—'Behold, what manner of love!'"

As we retire from that manger and stable, that aged
Christian puts his hand on my shoulder and says, "Young
man, I have often been to Bethlehem. It was a much-loved

haunt of mine before you were born. And there is one sweet lesson I have learned there which I should like to pass on to you. The Infinite became finite. The Almighty consented to become weak. He that upheld all things by the word of His power, willingly became helpless. He that spoke all worlds into existence, resigned for a while even the power of speech! In all these things, He fulfilled the will of His Father, so be not you afraid, nor surprised with any amazement if you should be dealt with in like manner, for His Father is also your Father. You who have reveled in the ancient settlements of the everlasting covenant, may yet have to hang feebly on the mercies of the hour. You have leaned on your Savior's breast at His table, but you may presently be so weak that you must rely on the nursing of a woman. Your tongue has been touched as with a coal from the heavenly altar, but your lips may yet be sealed as are those of an infant. If you should sink still deeper in humiliation, you will never reach the depth to which Jesus descended in this one act of His condescension." "True, true," I replied, "my young Brother hinted at the wondrous condescension of the Son of God. You have explained it to me more fully."

Thus, beloved, I have endeavored to carry out my purpose of going to Bethlehem with five separate companions—all representative persons. Alas that some of you are not represented by any one of these characters! "Is it nothing to you, all you that pass by?" Care you not for this blessed Nativity which marked of old, "the fullness of time"? If you die without a knowledge of this mystery, your lives will indeed be a fearful blank and your eternal portion will be truly terrible!

VI. Give me your earnest attention a little longer while I try to change the line of meditation. It may please God that while I attempt to conduct a whole family to Bethlehem, some hearts which have thus far resisted all my appeals may yet yield to the Lord Jesus Christ!

A familiar picture will serve my purpose. Imagine this to be Christmas Eve and that a Christian father has all his household gathered with him around the fire. Desirous of blending instruction with pleasure, he proposes that "the birth of Christ" shall be the subject of their conversation— that every one of the children shall say something about it and he will preach them a short sermon on each of their remarks. He calls Mary, their servant, into the room. And when all are comfortably seated they commence.

1. After a simple sketch of the facts, the father turns to his youngest boy and asks, "What have you to say, Willy?" The little fellow, who is just old enough to go to the Sunday school, repeats two lines that he has learned to sing there—many of you, no doubt, know them—

"Jesus Christ, my Lord and Savior,
Once became a child like me."

"Good, my dear," says the father—"once became a child like me. Yes. Jesus was born into the world as other little babies are born. He was as little, as delicate, as weak as other infants and needed to be nursed as they do—

"'Almighty God became a man,
A baby like others seen—
As small in size, and weak of frame,
As babies have always been.

From thence He grew an infant mild,
By fair and due degrees
And then became a bigger child,
And sat on Mary's knee.

'At first held up for need of strength,
In time alone He ran.
Then grew a boy. A lad—at length
A Youth—at last, a man.'

"It is wrong to draw pictures of the little Jesus and then say that they are like Him. Wicked idolaters do that. But we ought to think of Jesus Christ as made in all things like unto His brethren. There was never a thing in which He was not like us, except that He had no sin. He used to eat, drink, sleep, wake, laugh, cry and hold onto His mother, just as other children do. So it is quite right for you, Willy, to say, 'once became a Child like me.'"

2. "Now, John," said the father, addressing a lad rather older, "what have you to say?" "Well, father," said John, "if Jesus Christ was like us in some things, I do not think He could have had so many comforts as we have—not such a nice nursery, nor such a snug bed. Was He not disturbed by the horses, and cows, and camels? It seems to me shocking that He had to live in a stable."

"That is a very proper remark, John," said his father. "We ought all of us to think how our blessed Lord cast in His lot with the poor. When those Wise Men came from the East, I daresay they were surprised, at first, to find that Jesus was a poor man's child. Yet they fell down and worshipped Him, they opened their treasury and present- ed to Him very costly gifts—gold, and frankincense, and myrrh. Ah, when the Son of God made that great stoop from Heaven to earth, He passed the glittering palaces of kings and the marble halls of the rich and the noble—to take up His abode in the lodgings of poverty. Still, He was 'born King of the Jews.' Now, John, did you ever read of a child being born a king before? Of course you nev- er did—children have been born princes and heirs to a throne—but no other than Jesus was ever born a King. The poverty of our Savior's circumstances is like a foil which sets off the glorious dignity of His Person. You have read of good kings, such as David, Hezekiah and Josiah, yet, if they had not been kings, we would never have heard of them. But it was quite otherwise with Jesus Christ. He was possessed of more true greatness in a stable than any other king ever possessed in a palace! But do not imagine it was only in His childhood that Jesus was the kinsman of the poor. When He grew up to be a Man, He said, 'The fox- es have holes, and the birds of the air have nests, but the Son of Man has nowhere to lay His head.' Do you know, my children, that our comforts were purchased at the ex- pense of His sufferings? 'He became poor that we, through His poverty, might be rich.' We ought, therefore, to thank and praise the blessed Jesus every time we remember how much worse off He was in this world than we are."

3. "It is your turn now," said the father, as he looked at his little daughter—an intelligent girl who was just be- ginning to be of some assistance to her mother in the dis- charge of her daily domestic duties. Poor girl, she mod- estly hung down her head, for she remembered, just then, how frequently little acts of carelessness had exposed her to tender but faithful rebukes from her parents. At last she said, "Oh, Father, how good Jesus Christ was! He never did anything wrong."

"Very true, my Love," the father replied. "It is a sweet subject for meditation that you suggest. His nature was sinless, His thoughts were pure, His heart was transparent and all His actions just and right. You have read of the lambs which Moses, in the Law, commanded the Jews to offer in sacrifice to God. They were all to be without spot or blemish—and if there had been one taint of impurity in the child that was born of Mary, He could never have been our Savior. Sometimes we think naughty thoughts and nobody knows it but God. And, sometimes, we do what is evil, but we are not found out. It was not so with the meek and lowly Savior—He never had even one fault! His delight was in the Law of the Lord and in that Law did He meditate day and night. Even when we do not commit any positive sin, we often forget to do our duty, but Jesus never did. He was like a tree planted by the rivers of water that brings forth its fruit in its season. He never disappointed any hopes that were set upon Him."

"There now," said the father, "we have already had three beautiful thoughts—Jesus Christ took our nature, He condescended to be very poor and He was without sin."

4. There was, in the room, a big boy who had just come home from boarding school to spend his Christmas holidays, so his father turned to this son and said, "Fred, we must hear your remark next." Very short, very significant was Master Fred's response—"that Child had a wonderful mind."

"Indeed He had," said the father, "and it would be well for all of us if that mind were in us which was also in Christ Jesus. His mind was infinite, for He took part in the eternal counsels of God. But I would rather suggest to you another line of thought—'In Him was Light.' The mind of Jesus was like light for its clearness and purity. We often see things through a misleading medium. We form wrong impressions which we find it trouble enough afterwards to correct. But Jesus was of quick understanding to discern between good and evil. His mind was never warped by prejudice. He saw things just as they are. Never had He to borrow other people's eyes—and the ideas hatched in other people's brains never guided His judgment. He had light in Himself and that light was the life of men, so capable was He of always instructing the ignorant and guiding their feet in the paths of peace. His heart was likewise pure and that has more to do with the development of the mind and the improvement of the understanding than we are apt to suppose. No corrupt imagination ever tarnished the brightness of His vision. He was always in harmony with God and always felt good-will toward man. You might well say, Fred, that He had a wonderful mind."

5. The children having each made some observation, the father next addressed Mary, the servant. "Do not be timid," he said, "but speak out and let us know your thoughts." "I was just a-thinking, Sir," said Mary, "how

humble it was of Him to take upon Himself the form of a Servant."

"Right, Mary, quite right. And it is always profitable to consider how Jesus came down to our low estate. We may well be reconciled to any 'lot' which Jesus voluntarily chose for Himself. But there is more in your remark, as applicable to Bethlehem and the Nativity, than you perhaps imagined, for, according to Dr. Kitto's account of the inn, or Caravanserai, it was the servant's place that the holy family occupied. Imagine now a square pile of strong and lofty walls, built of brick upon a basement of stone with one great archway entrance. These walls enclose a large open area with a well in the middle. In the center is an inner quadrangle consisting of a raised platform on all four sides covered with a kind of piazza. And then, in the wall behind, there are small doors leading to the little cells which form the lodgings. Such we may suppose to have been the 'inn' in which there was 'no room' for Mary and Joseph. Now for a description of the stable. It is formed of a covered avenue between the back wall of the lodging apartments and the outer wall of the whole building—thus it is on a level with the court and three or four feet below the raised platform. The side walls of those cells, in the inner quadrangle, projecting behind into the courtyard, form recesses, or stalls, which servants and muleteers used for shelter in bad weather. Joseph and Mary seem to have found a retreat in one of these. There, it is supposed, the infant Jesus was born. And if it is so, how literally true is it that He took on Him the form of a servant and occupied the servant's apartment!"

6. Once more the father seeks a fresh text and, looking at his wife, he says, "My dear, you have taken a quiet interest in our conversations this evening. Let us now hear your reflection. I am sure you can say something we shall all be pleased to hear." The mother looked absorbed in thought. She appeared to have a vivid picture of the whole scene before her and her eyes kindled as if she could actually see the little darling lying in the manger. She spoke most naturally and most maternally, too. "What a lovely child! And yet," she added with a deep sigh, "He who is thus fairer than the children of men in His cradle, after a few short years was so overwhelmed with anxiety, suffering and anguish, that His visage was more marred than that of any other man! And His form more than that of the sons of men."

A pensive sadness stole over every countenance as
that godly mother offered her reflections. Woman's tenderness seemed to be sanctified by divine grace in her
heart and to give forth its richest fragrance. The father
presently broke the stillness as he said, "Ah, my Love,
you have spoken best of all! His heart was broken with
reproach! That humble birth was but the prelude to a life
still more humble and a death even more abased! Your
feelings, my love, are most precious evidence of your close
relationship to Him—

"'A faithful friend of grief partakes;
But union can be none
Betwixt a heart that melts like wax
And hearts as hard as stone.

Betwixt a head diffusing blood
And members sound and whole,
Betwixt an agonizing God
And an unfeeling soul.

7. "To close up now," said the father, glancing round
with animated expression upon his household, "I suppose
you will expect a few words from me. Much as I like your
mother's observations, I think it would be hardly right, on
such an auspicious day, to finish with anything melan-
choly and sad. You know that fathers are generally most
thoughtful about the prospects of their children. I can look
at you boys and think, 'Never mind if you have a few
hardships so long as you can struggle successfully against
them.' Well now, I have been picturing to myself the manger, the baby that lay in it, and

Mary, His mother watching lovingly over Him. And
I'll tell you what I thought. Those little hands will one day
grasp the scepter of universal empire! Those little arms will
one day grapple with the monster, 'Death,' and destroy
it! Those little feet shall tread on the serpent's neck and
crush that old deceiver's head! Yes, and that little tongue
which has not yet learned to articulate a word shall, before
long, pour from His sweet lips such streams of eloquence
as shall fertilize the minds of the whole human race and
infuse His teaching into the literature of the world! And
again, a little while, and that tongue shall pronounce the
judgments of Heaven on the destinies of all mankind!

"We have all thought it wonderful that the God of
Glory should stoop so low, but we shall one day think it

more wonderful that the Man of Sorrows should be exalted so high! Earth could find no place too base for Him—
Heaven will scarcely find a place lofty enough for Him! If
there is just this one thing to be said about Jesus Christ, He
is 'the same yesterday, and today, and forever.' We may
change with circumstances—Jesus never did and never
will! When we look at Him in the manger, we may say,
'He is The Wonderful, The Counselor, The Mighty God.'
And when we see Him exalted to His Father's right hand,
we may exclaim, 'Behold the Man!'—

> "'His human heart He still retains
> Though enthroned in highest bliss
> And feels each tempted member's pains,
> For our affliction's His.'"

So closed the series of observations by the various
members of a Christian family around the Christmas fire.
The father said it was time to retire. And he bade them all,
'good night.'" And as the father said, so say I, "Good night
and God bless you all!" Amen.

IV. HOLY WORK FOR CHRISTMAS

*"And when they had seen it, they made known abroad
the saying which was told them concerning this Child.
And all they that heard it wondered at those things which
were told them by the shepherds. But Mary kept all these
things and pondered them in her heart. And the shepherds
returned, glorifying and praising God for all the things
that they had heard and seen, as it was told unto them."*
Luke 2:17-20.

Every season has its own proper fruit—apples for autumn,
holly berries for Christmas. The earth brings forth according to the period of the year and with man there is a time
for every purpose under Heaven. At this season the world
is engaged in congratulating itself and in expressing its
complimentary wishes for the good of its citizens. Let me
suggest extra and more solid work for Christians. As we
think, today, of the birth of the Savior, let us aspire after
a fresh birth of the Savior in our hearts—that as He is already "formed in us the hope of glory," we may be "renewed in the spirit of our minds"—that we may go again
to the Bethlehem of our spiritual nativity and do our first
works, enjoy our first loves and feast with Jesus as we did
in the holy, happy, heavenly days of our espousals.

Let us go to Jesus with something of that youthful
freshness and excessive delight which was so manifest in
us when we looked to Him at first. Let Him be crowned
anew by us, for He is still adorned with the dew of His
youth and remains "the same yesterday, today and forever." The citizens of Durham, though they dwell not far
from the Scotch border, and consequently in the olden
times were frequently liable to be attacked, were exempt-
ed from the toils of war because there was a cathedral
within their walls and they were set aside to the bishop's
service, being called in the olden times by the name of
"holy work-folk."

Now, we citizens of the New Jerusalem, having the
Lord Jesus in our midst, may well excuse ourselves from

the ordinary ways of celebrating this season. And considering ourselves to be "holy work-folk," we may keep it, after a different sort from other men, in holy contemplation and in blessed service of that gracious God whose unspeakable gift the new-born King is to us.

I selected this text this morning because it seemed to indicate to me four ways of serving God, four methods of executing holy work and exercising Christian thought. Each of the verses sets before us a different way of sacred service. Some, it appears, published abroad the news, told to others what they had seen and heard. Some wondered with a holy marveling and astonishment. One, at least, according to the third verse, pondered, meditated, thought upon these things. And others, in the fourth place, glorified God and gave Him praise. I know not which of these four did God the best service, but I think if we could combine all these mental emotions and outward exercises we should be sure to praise God after a most godly and acceptable fashion.

I. To begin then, in the first place, we find that some celebrated the Savior's birth by publishing abroad what they had heard and seen. And truly we may say of them that they had something to rehearse in men's ears well worth the telling! That for which Prophets and kings had waited long had at last arrived and arrived to them! They had found out the answer to the perpetual riddle. They might have run through the streets with the ancient philosopher, crying, "Eureka! Eureka!" for their discovery was far superior to his.

They had found out no solution to a mechanical problem or metaphysical dilemma. Their discovery was second to none ever made by men in real value, since it has been like the leaves of the Tree of Life to heal the nations and a river of Water of Life to make glad the city of God! They had seen angels! They had heard them sing a song all strange and new. They had seen more than angels—they had beheld the angel's King, the Angel of the Covenant whom we delight in! They had heard the music of Heaven, and when near that manger, the ear of their faith had heard the music of earth's hope, a mystic harmony which should ring all down the ages—the sweet melody of hearts attuned to praise the Lord and the glorious swell of the holy joy of God and man rejoicing in glad accord.

They had seen God Incarnate—such a sight that he who gazes on it must feel his tongue unloosed—unless, indeed, an unspeakable astonishment should make him dumb! Be silent when their eyes had seen such a vision? Impossible! To the first person they met outside that lowly stable door they began to tell their matchless tale and they wearied not till nightfall, crying, "Come and worship! Come and worship Christ, the new-born King!" As for us, Beloved, have we also not something to relate which demands utterance? If we talk of Jesus, who can blame us? This, indeed, might make the tongue of him that sleeps to move—the mystery of God Incarnate, for our sake bleeding and dying—that we might neither bleed nor die! God Incarnate descending that we might ascend! Wrapped in swaddling cloths that we might be unwrapped of the grave clothes of corruption!

Here is such a story, so profitable to all hearers that he who repeats it the most often does best, and he who speaks the least has most reason to accuse himself for sinful silence. They had something to tell and that something had in it the inimitable blending which is the secret sign and royal march of divine authorship—a peerless marrying of sublimity and simplicity! Angels singing—singing to shepherds! Heaven bright with glory! Bright at midnight! God! A Babe! The Infinite! An infant of a span long!! The Ancient of Days! Born of a woman! What more simple than the inn, the manger, a carpenter, a carpenter's wife, a child?

What more sublime than a "multitude of the heavenly host" waking the midnight with their joyous song and God Himself in human flesh made manifest? A child is but an ordinary sight—but what a marvel to see that Word which was "in the beginning with God, tabernacling among us that we might behold His Glory"—the Glory as of the only begotten of the Father, full of grace and truth? Brethren, we have a tale to tell, as simple as sublime. What simpler?—"Believe and live." What more sublime?—"Was in Christ reconciling the world unto Himself!" A system of salvation so wonderful that angelic minds cannot but adore as they meditate upon it. And yet so simple that the children in the temple may fitly hymn its virtues as they sing. "Hosanna! Blessed is He that comes in the name of the Lord."

What a splendid combining of the sublime and the simple have we in the great atonement offered by the incarnate Savior! Oh make known to all men this saving truth of God! The shepherds need no excuse for making everywhere the announcement of the Savior's birth, for what they told they first received from Heaven! Their news was not muttered in their ears by Sybilline oracles, nor brought to light by philosophic research. It was not conceived in poetry nor found as treasure trove among the volumes of the ancient. It was revealed to them by that notable Gospel preacher who led the angelic host and testified, "Unto you is born this day, in the city of David, a Savior, which is Christ the Lord."

When Heaven entrusts a man with a merciful Revelation, he is bound to deliver the good tidings to others. What? Keep that a secret whose utterance eternal mercy makes to charm the midnight air? To what purpose were angels sent if the message were not to be spread abroad? According to the teaching of our own beloved Lord we must not be silent, for He bids us, "What you hear in secret, that reveal you in public. And what I tell you in the ear in closets, that proclaim you upon the housetops." Beloved, you have heard a voice from Heaven—you twice-born men, begotten again unto a lively hope—you have heard the Spirit of God bearing witness of God's truth with you and teaching you of heavenly things. You, then, must keep this Christmas by telling to your fellow men what God's own holy Spirit has seen fit to reveal to you!

But though the shepherds told what they heard from Heaven, remember that they spoke of what they had seen below. They had, by observation, made those truths of God most surely their own which had first been spoken to them by Revelation. No man can speak of the things of God with any success until the doctrine which he finds in the Bible, he finds, also, in his heart. We must bring down the mystery and make it plain by knowing, and by the teaching of the Holy Spirit its practical power on the heart and conscience. My brethren, the Gospel which we preach is most surely revealed to us by the Lord. But, moreover, our hearts have tried and proved, have grasped, have felt, have realized its truth and power!

If we have not been able to understand its heights and depths, yet we have felt its mystic power upon our heart and spirit. It has revealed sin to us plainly. It has revealed to us our pardon. It has killed the reigning power of sin. It has given us Christ to reign over us and the Holy Spirit to dwell within our bodies as in a temple. Now we must speak! I do not urge any of you to speak of Jesus who merely know the Word as you find it in the Bible—your teaching can have but little power. But I do speak earnestly to you who know its mighty influence upon the heart, who have not only heard of the babe but have seen Him in the manger.

I speak to those who have taken Him up in your arms and received Him as being born to you, a Savior to you—Christ the Anointed—Jesus, the Savior from sin, for you. Beloved, can you do otherwise than speak of the things which you have seen and heard? God has made you to taste and to handle of this good word of life and you must not, you dare not hold your peace! You must tell friends and neighbors what you have felt within.

These were shepherds, unlettered men. I will warrant you they could not read in a book. There is no probability that they even knew a single letter. They were shepherds, but they preached right well. And, my brethren, whatever some may think, preaching is not to be confined to those learned gentlemen who have taken their degrees at Oxford or at Cambridge, or at any college or university. It is true that learning need not be an impediment to grace and may be a fitting weapon in a gracious hand. But often the grace of God has glorified itself by the plain clear way in which unlettered men have understood the Gospel and have proclaimed it.

I would not mind asking the whole world to find a Master of Arts now living who has brought more souls to Christ Jesus than Richard Weaver. If the whole bench of bishops have done a tenth as much in the way of soul-winning as that one man, it is more than most of us give them credit for. Let us give to our God all the glory, but still let us not deny the fact that this sinner saved, with the brogue of the coal miner still about him, fresh from the coal pit, tells the story of the cross, by God's grace, in such a way that right reverend fathers in God might humbly sit at his feet to learn the way to reach the heart and melt the stubborn soul!

It is true an uneducated brother is not fitted for all work—he has his own sphere—but he is quite able to tell of what he has seen and heard. And so it strikes me, is every man in a measure. If you have seen Jesus and heard His saving voice. If you have received truth as from the Lord. If you have felt its tremendous power as coming from God to you, and if you have experienced its might upon your own spirit—why you can surely tell out what God has written within! If you cannot get beyond that into the deeper mysteries, into the more knotty points, well, well, there are some who can, and so you need not be uneasy. But you can at least reveal the first and foundational truths and they are by far the most important!

If you cannot speak in the pulpit. If as yet your cheek would mantle with a blush and your tongue would refuse to do her office in the presence of many, there are your children! You are not ashamed to speak before them! There is the little cluster round the hearth on Christmas night. There is the little congregation in the workshop. There is a little audience somewhere to whom you might tell out of Jesus' love to lost ones. Do not get beyond what you know. Do not plunge into what you have not experienced—for if you do, you will be out of your depth—and then very soon you will be floundering and making confusion worse confounded. Go as far as you know. And since you know yourself to be a sinner—and Jesus a savior, and a great one, too—talk about those two matters and good will come of it! Beloved, each one, in his own position, tell what you have heard and seen! Publish that abroad among the sons of men.

But were the shepherds authorized? It is a great thing to be authorized! Unauthorized ministers are most shameful intruders! Unordained men who are not in the Apostolic succession entering the pulpit—very horrible—very horrible indeed! The Puseyite mind utterly fails to fathom the depth of horror which is contained in the idea of an unauthorized man preaching and a man out of the Apostolic succession daring to teach the way of salvation! To me this horror seems very much like a schoolboy's fright at a hobgoblin which his fears had conjured up. I think if I saw a man slip through the ice into a cold grave and I could rescue him from drowning it would not be so very horrible to me to be the means of saving him, though I may not be employed by the Royal Humane Society.

I imagine if I saw a fire and heard a poor woman scream at an upper window and likely to be burned alive, if I should wheel the fire escape up to the window and preserve her life, it would not be so very dreadful a matter though I might not belong to the regular fire brigade. If a company of brave volunteers should chase an enemy out of their own county, I do not know that it would be anything so shocking although a whole army of mercenaries might be neglecting their work in obedience to some venerable military rubric which rendered them incapable of effective service. But mark you, the shepherds and others like them are in the Apostolic succession and they are authorized by divine ordinance—for every man who hears the Gospel is authorized to tell it to others.

Do you want authority? Here it is in strong confirmation from Holy Writ—"Let him that hears say, Come"— that is, let every man who truly hears the Gospel bid others come to drink of the water of life. This is all the warrant you require for preaching the Gospel according to your ability. It is not every man who has ability to preach the Word. And it is not every man that we should like to hear preach it in the great congregation, for if all were mouth, what a great vacuum the Church would be! Yet every Christian in some method should deliver the glad tidings. Our wise God takes care that liberty of prophesying shall not run to riot, for He does not give efficient pastoral and ministerial gifts to every many. Yet every man, according to his gifts, let him minister! Every one of you, though not in the pulpit, yet in the pew, in the workshop—somewhere, anywhere, everywhere—make known the savor of the Lord Jesus. And let this be your authority—"Let him that hears, say, Come."

I never thought of asking any authority for crying, "Fire!" When I saw a house burning, I never dreamed of seeking any authority for doing my best to rescue a poor perishing fellow man. Nor do I mean to seek it now! All the authority you want, any of you, is not the authority which can stream from prelates decorated with long sleeves—but the authority which comes directly from the great head of the church who gives authority to every one of those who hear the Gospel to teach every man, his fellow, saying, "Know the Lord." Here, dear brethren, is one way for you to keep a right holy, and in some sense, a right merry Christmas! Imitate these humble men, of whom it is said, "When they had seen it they made known abroad the saying which was told them concerning this Child."

II. We set before you, now, another mode of keeping Christmas by holy wonder, admiration, and adoration. "And all they that heard it wondered at those things which were told them by the shepherds." We shall have little to say of those persons who merely wondered and did nothing more. Many are set a wondering by the Gospel. They are content to hear it, pleased to hear it—though not, to them, in itself something new—yet there are new ways of putting it and they are glad to be refreshed with the variety. The preacher's voice is to them as the sound of one that gives a goodly tune upon an instrument. They are glad to listen. They are not skeptics. They do not cavil. They raise no difficulties. They just say to themselves, "It is an excellent Gospel. It is a wonderful plan of salvation. Here is most astonishing love, most extraordinary condescension." Sometimes they marvel that these things should be told them by shepherds. They can hardly understand how unlearned and ignorant men should speak of these things! And they marvel how such things should ever get into these shepherds' heads—where they learned them, how it is that they seem so earnest about them—what kind of operation they must have passed through to be able to speak as they do. But after holding up their hands and opening their mouths for about nine days, the wonder subsides and they go their way and think no more about it. There are many of you who are set to wondering whenever you see a work of God in your district. You hear of somebody converted who was a very extraordinary sinner and you say, "It is very wonderful!" There is a revival. You happen to be present at one of the meetings when the Spirit of God is working gloriously—you say, "Well, this is a singular thing! Very astonishing!" Even the newspapers can afford a corner, at times, for very great and extraordinary works of God the Holy Spirit! But then all emotion ends—it is all wondering and nothing more. Now, I trust it will not be so with any of us—that we shall not think of the Savior and of the doctrines of the Gospel which He came to preach simply with amazement and astonishment—for this will work us but little good.

On the other hand, there is another mode of wondering which is akin to adoration, if it is not adoration, itself. I think it would be very difficult to draw a line between holy wonder and real worship. When the soul is overwhelmed with the majesty of God's Glory, though it may not express itself in song, or even utter its voice with bowed head in humble prayer, yet it silently adores. I am inclined to think that the astonishment which sometimes seizes upon the human intellect at the remembrance of God's greatness and goodness is, perhaps, the purest form of adoration which ever rises from mortal men to the throne of the Most High. This kind of wonder I recommend to those of you who, from the quietness and solitariness of your lives, are scarcely able to imitate the shepherds in telling out the tale to others—you can at least fill up the circle of the worshippers before the throne by wondering at what God has done.

Let me suggest to you that holy wonder at what God has done should be very natural to you. That God should consider His fallen creature, man—and instead of sweeping him away with the besom of destruction—should devise a wonderful scheme for his redemption and that He should, Himself, undertake to be man's Redeemer and to pay his ransom price, is, indeed, marvelous! Probably it is most marvelous to you in its relation to yourself, that you should be redeemed by blood! That God should forsake the thrones and royalties above to suffer ignominiously below for you! If you know yourself you can never see any adequate motive or reason in your own flesh for such a deed as this. "Why such love to me?" you will say. If David, sitting in his house, could only say, "Who am I, O Lord God, and what is my house, that You have brought me up hitherto?" what should you and I say? Had we been the most meritorious of individuals and had unceasingly kept the Lord's commands we could not have deserved such a priceless gift as Incarnation! But, sinners, offenders who revolted and went from God further and further, what shall we say of this incarnate God dying for us? "Herein is love, not that we loved God but that God loved us." Let your soul lose itself in wonder, for wonder, dear friends, is in this way a very practical emotion! Holy wonder will lead you to grateful worship! Being astonished at what God has done, you will pour out your soul with astonishment at the foot of the golden throne with the song,

> "Blessing and honor and glory and majesty and power and
> dominion and might be unto Him who sits on the Throne
> and does these great things for me."

Filled with this wonder it will cause you a godly watchfulness. You will be afraid to sin against such love as this! Feeling the presence of the mighty God in the gift of His dear Son, you will take off your shoes because the place where you stand is holy ground. You will be moved at the same time to a glorious hope! If Jesus has given Himself to you. If He has done this marvelous thing on your behalf, you will feel that heaven itself is not too great for your expectation and that the rivers of pleasure at God's right hand are not too sweet or too deep for you to drink! Who can be astonished at anything when he has once been astonished at the manger and the cross? What is there wonderful left after one has seen the Savior? The nine wonders of the world? Why, you may put them all into a nutcracker and a child's art can excel them all! This one wonder is not the wonder of earth only, but of heaven and earth and even hell itself! It is not the wonder of the olden time, but the wonder of all time and the wonder of eternity. They who see human wonders a few times finally cease to be astonished. The noblest pile that architect ever raised finally fails to impress the onlooker—but not so this marvelous temple of incarnate Deity! The more we look the more we are astonished! The more we become accustomed to it, the more we have a sense of its surpassing splendor of love and grace! There is more of God, let us say, to be seen in the manger and the cross, than in the sparkling stars above, the rolling deep below, the towering mountain, the teeming valleys, the abodes of life, or the abyss of death! Let us, then, spend some choice hours of this festive season in holy wonder—such as will produce gratitude, worship, love and confidence.

III. A third manner of holy work, namely, her heart pondering and preserving, you will find in the next verse. One at least and let us hope there were others, or at any rate let us ourselves be the others—one kept all these things and pondered them in her heart. She wondered—she did more—she pondered. You will observe there was an exercise on the part of this blessed woman of the three great parts of her being—her memory—she kept all these things. Her affections—she kept them in her heart. Her intellect—she pondered them, considered them, weighed them, turned them over—so that memory, affection and understanding were all exercised about these things. We delight to see this in Mary, but we are not at all surprised when we recollect that she was, in some sense, the most concerned of all on earth—for it was of her that Jesus Christ had been born. Those who come nearest to Jesus and enter the most closely into fellowship with Him will be sure to be the most engrossed with Him. Certain persons are best esteemed at a distance, but not the Savior! When you shall have known Him to the very fullest, then shall you love Him with the love which passes knowledge. You shall comprehend the heights and depths and lengths and breadths of His love. And when you shall do so, then your own love shall swell beyond all length and breadth, all height and depth. The birth most concerned Mary and therefore she was the most impressed with it. Note the way in which her concern was shown—she was a woman and the grace which shines best in the female is not bold-ness—that belongs to the masculine mind. Affectionate modesty is a feminine beauty, and from now we do not read so much of her telling abroad as pondering within. No doubt she had her circle and her word to speak in it, but for the most part she, like another Mary, sat still in the house. She worked, but her work was most directly for Him, her heart's joy and delight. Like other children, the holy Child needed care, which only a mother's hand and heart could exercise. She was, therefore, engrossed with Him. O blessed engrossment! Sweet engagement!

Count not that to be unacceptable service which oc-cupies itself rather with Jesus than with His disciples or His wandering sheep. That woman who broke the alabas-ter box and poured the ointment upon our Jesus Himself was faulted by Judas. And even the rest of the disciples thought that the poor had lost a benefit, but "she has worked a good work on Me" was the Savior's answer. I desire to bring you to this thought—if during this season you retiring, quiet ones, cannot speak to others, or have no desirable opportunity or suitable gift for that work—you may sit still with Jesus and honor Him in peace. Mary took the Lord in her arms. Oh that you may bear Him in yours! She executed works directly for His person directly—im-itate her! You can love Him, bless Him, praise Him, study Him, ponder Him, comprehend His character, study the types that set Him forth and imitate His life! And in this way, though your worship will not blaze forth among the sons of men and scarcely benefit them as some other forms of work, yet it will both benefit you and be acceptable to your Lord. Beloved, remember what you have heard of Christ and what He has done for you! Make your heart the golden cup to hold the rich remembrances of His past loving-kindness! Make it a pot of manna to preserve the heavenly bread on which saints have fed in days gone by. Let your memory treasure up everything about Christ which you have either heard, or felt, or known! And then let your fond affections hold Him fast forevermore. Love Him! Pour out that alabaster box of your heart, and let all the precious ointment of your affections come streaming on His feet. If you cannot do it with joy, do it sorrowfully: wash His feet with tears, wipe them with the hairs of your head—but do love Him—love the blessed Son of God, your ever tender friend. Let your intellect be exercised

concerning the Lord Jesus. Turn over and over by meditation what you read. Do not be loiter men—do not stop
at the surface—dive into the depths. Be not as the swallow which touches the brook with her wing, but as the fish
which penetrates the lowest wave. Drink deep draughts of
love! Do not sip and away—but dwell at the well as Isaac
did at the well Lahai-roi. Abide with your Lord—let Him
not be to you as a wayfaring man that tarries for a night,
but constrain Him, saying, "Abide with us, for the day is
far spent." Hold Him and do not let Him go! The word
"ponder," as you know, means to weigh. Make ready the
scales of judgment. Oh, but where are the scales that can
weigh the Lord Christ? "He takes up the isles as a very little thing"—who shall take Him up? "He weighs the mountains in scales." In what scales shall we weigh Him? Be
it so, if your understanding cannot comprehend, let your
affections apprehend. And if your spirit cannot compass
the Lord Jesus in the arms of its understanding, let it embrace Him in the arms of your affection. Oh, beloved, here
is blessed Christmas work for you, if, like Mary, you lay
up all these things in your heart and ponder upon them.

IV. The last piece of holy Christmas work is to come.
"The shepherds returned," we read in the twentieth verse,
"Glorifying and praising god for all the things that they
had heard and seen, as it was told unto them."

Returned to what? Returned to business to look after
the lambs and sheep again. Then if we desire to glorify
God we need not give up our business.

Some people get the notion into their heads that the
only way in which they can live for God is by becoming
ministers, missionaries, or Bible women. Alas, how many
of us would be shut out from any opportunity of magni-
fying the Most High if this were the case? The shepherds
went back to the sheep pens glorifying and praising God!
Beloved, it is not office, it is earnestness; it is not position, it
is divine grace which will enable us to glorify God. God is
most surely glorified in that cobbler's stall where the godly worker, as he plies the awl, sings of the Savior's love,
yes, glorified far more than in many a cathedral where of-
ficial religiousness performs its scanty duties. The name
of Jesus is glorified by yonder carter as he drives his horse
and blesses his God, or speaks to his fellow laborer by the
roadside as much as by yonder divine who, throughout
the country like Boanerges, is thundering out the Gospel!
God is glorified by our abiding in our vocation. Take care

you do not fall out of the path of duty by leaving your calling, and take care you do not dishonor your profession while in it! Think not much of yourselves, but do not think too little of your callings. There is no trade which is not sanctified by the Gospel. If you turn to the Bible, you will find the most menial forms of labor have been in some way or other connected either with the most daring deeds of faith, or else with persons whose lives have been otherwise illustrious. Keep to your calling, brother, keep to your calling! Whatever God has made you, when He calls you, abide in that, unless you are quite sure—mind that—unless you are quite sure that He calls you to something else. The shepherds glorified God though they went to their trade.

They glorified God though they were shepherds. As we remarked, they were not men of learning. So far from having an extensive library full of books, it is probable they could not read a word. Yet they glorified God. This takes away all excuse for you good people who say, "I am no scholar. I never had any education. I never went even to a Sunday school." Ah, but if your heart is right, you can glorify God. Never mind, Sarah, do not be cast down because you know so little. Learn more if you can, but make good use of what you do know. Never mind, John, it is indeed a pity that you should have had to toil so early, as not to have acquired even the rudiments of knowledge—but do not think that you cannot glorify God. If you would praise God, live a holy life! You can do that by His grace, at any rate, without scholarship. If you would do good to others, be good yourself. And that is a way which is as open to the most illiterate as it is to the best taught. Be of good courage! Shepherds glorified God and so may you. Remember there is one thing in which they had a preference over the wise men. The wise men wanted a star to lead them. The shepherds did not. The wise men went wrong even with a star—they stumbled into Jerusalem. The shepherds went straight away to Bethlehem. Simple minds sometimes find a glorified Christ where learned heads, much puzzled with their lore, miss Him. A good doctor used to say, "Lo, these simpletons have entered into the kingdom, while we learned men have been fumbling for the latch." It is often so. And so, you simple minds, be ye comforted and glad.

The way in which these shepherds honored God is worth noticing. They did it by praising Him. Let us think more of sacred song than we sometimes do. When the song is bursting in full chorus from the thousands in this house, it is but a noise in the ear of some men—but inasmuch as many true hearts, touched with the love of Jesus, are keeping pace with their tongues—it is not a mere noise in God's esteem. There is a sweet music in it that makes glad His ear. What is the great ultimatum of all Christian effort? When I stood here the other morning preaching the Gospel, my mind was fully exercised with the winning of souls. But I seemed, while preaching, to get beyond that. I thought, Well, that is not the chief end after all—the chief end is to glorify God and even the saving of sinners is sought by the right-minded as the means to that end. Then it struck me all of a sudden, if in Psalm singing and hymn singing we do really glorify God, we are doing more than in the preaching because we are not then in the means— we are close upon the great end itself. If we praise God with heart and tongue we glorify Him in the surest possible manner—we are really glorifying Him then! "Whoever offers praise glorifies Me," says the Lord. Sing, then, my brethren! Sing not only when you are together, but sing alone! Cheer your labor with Psalms and hymns and spiritual songs. Make glad the family with sacred music! We sing too little, I am sure, yet the revival of religion has always been attended with the revival of Christian psalmody. Luther's translations of the Psalms were of as much service as Luther's discussions and controversies. And the hymns of Charles Wesley and Cennick and Toplady and Newton and Cowper aided as much in the quickening of spiritual life in England as the preaching of John Wesley and George Whitefield. We want more singing. Sing more and murmur less, sing more and slander less, sing more and cavil less, sing more and mourn less. God grant us today, as these shepherds did, to glorify God by praising Him.

I have not quite done with them. What was the subject of their praise? It appears that they praised God for what they had heard. If we think of it, there is good reason for blessing God every time we hear a Gospel sermon. What would souls in hell give if they could hear the Gospel once more and be on terms in which salvation grace might come to them? What would dying men give whose tune is all but over if they could once more come to the house of God and have another warning and another invitation? My brethren, what would you give, sometimes, when you are shut up by sickness and cannot meet with the great congregation—when your heart and your flesh cry out for the living God? Well, praise God for what you have heard. You have heard the faults of the preacher—let him mourn them. You have heard his Master's message. Do you bless God for that? Scarcely will you ever hear a sermon which may not make you sing if you are in a right frame of mind. George Herbert says, "Praying is the end of preaching." So it is, but praising is its end, too. Praise God that you hear there is a Savior. Praise God that you hear that the plan of salvation is very simple. Praise God that you have a Savior for your own soul. Praise God that you are pardoned, that you are saved.

Praise Him for what you have heard, but observe, they also praised God for what they had seen. Look at the twentieth verse—"heard and seen." There is the sweetest music—what we have experienced, what we have felt within, what we have made our own—the things that we have made touching the King! Mere hearing may make some music, but the soul of song must come from seeing with the eye of faith. And, dear friends, you who have seen with that God-given eyesight—I pray you, let not your tongues be steeped in sinful silence! Speak loudly to the praise of sovereign grace!

One point for which they praised God was the agreement between what they had heard and what they had seen. Observe the last sentence. "As it was told unto them." Have you not found the Gospel to be in yourselves just what the Bible said it would be? Jesus said He would give you grace—have you not had it? He promised you rest—have you not received it? He said that you should have joy and comfort and life through believing in Him—have you not had all these? Are not His ways ways of pleasantness and His paths, paths of peace? Surely you can say with the queen of Sheba, "The half has not been told me." I have found Christ more sweet than His servants could set Him forth as being. I looked upon the likeness as they painted it, but it was a mere daub as compared with Himself—the King in His beauty. I have heard of the goodly land, but oh, it flows with milk and honey more richly and sweetly than men were ever able to tell me in their best trim for speech. Surely what we have seen keeps pace with what we have heard. Let us, then, glorify and praise God for what He has done.

This word to those who are not yet converted and I have done. I do not think you can begin at the seventeenth verse, but I wish you would begin at the eighteenth. You cannot begin at the seventeenth—you cannot tell to others what you have not felt. Do not try it. Neither teach in the Sunday school, nor attempt to preach if you are not converted. Unto the wicked, God says, "What have you to do to declare My statutes?" But I would to God you would begin with the eighteenth verse—wondering! Wondering that you are spared—wondering that you are out of hell—wondering that still does His good Spirit strive with the chief of sinners! Wonder that this morning the Gospel should have a word for you after all your rejections of it and sins against God. I should like you to begin there because then I should have good hope that you would go on to the next verse and change the first letter and so go from wondering to pondering. Oh sinner, I wish you would ponder the doctrines of the cross. Think of your sin, God's wrath, judgment, Hell, your Savior's blood, God's love, forgiveness, acceptance, heaven—think on these things. Go from wondering to pondering. And then I would to God you could go on to the next verse, from pondering to glorifying. Take Christ, look to Him, trust Him! Then sing, "I am forgiven," and go your way a believing sinner and therefore a saved sinner, washed in the blood, and clean. Then go back, after that, to the seventeenth verse and begin to tell others.

But as for you Christians who are saved, I want you to begin this very afternoon at the seventeenth—

> "Then will I tell to sinners round
> What a dear Savior I have found!
> I'll point to Your redeeming blood,
> And say—'Behold, the way to God!'"

Then when the day is over, get up to your chambers and wonder, admire and adore. Spend half an hour also like Mary in pondering and treasuring up the day's work and the day's hearing in your hearts and then close all with that which never must close—go on tonight, tomorrow and all the days of your life, glorifying and praising God for all the things that you have seen and heard. May the Master bless you for Jesus Christ's sake. Amen.

V. THE FIRST CHRISTMAS CAROL

"Glory to God in the highest, and on earth peace, good
will toward men."
Luke 2:14

It is superstitious to worship angels; it is but proper to love
them. Although it would be a high sin, and an act of mis-
demeanor against the sovereign court of heaven to pay the
slightest adoration to the mightiest angel, yet it would be
unkind and unseemly, if we did not give to holy angels
a place in our heart's warmest love. In fact, he that con-
templates the character of angels, and marks their many
deeds of sympathy with men, and kindness towards them,
cannot resist the impulse of his nature—the impulse of
love towards them. The one incident in angelic history, to
which our text refers, is enough to weld our hearts to them
for ever. How free from envy the angels were! Christ did
not come from heaven to save their compeers when they
fell. When Satan, the mighty angel, dragged with him a
third part of the stars of heaven, Christ did not stoop from
his throne to die for them; but he left them to be reserved
in chains and darkness until the last great day. Yet angels
did not envy men. Though they remembered that he took
not up angels, yet they did not murmur when he took up
the seed of Abraham; and though the blessed master had
never condescended to take the angel's form, they did not
think it beneath them to express their joy when they found
him arrayed in the body of an infant. How free, too, they
were from pride! They were not ashamed to come and tell
the news to humble shepherds. Methinks they had as much
joy in pouring out their songs that night before the shepherds, who were watching with their flocks, as they would
have had if they had been commanded by their master to
sing their hymn in the halls of Caesar. Mere men—men
possessed with pride, think it a fine thing to preach before
kings and princes; and think it great condescension now
and then to have to minister to the humble crowd. Not so
the angels. They stretched their willing wings, and gladly

sped from their bright seats above, to tell the shepherds
on the plain by night, the marvelous story of an incarnate
God. And mark how well they told the story, and surely
you will love them! Not with the stammering tongue of
him that tells a tale in which he hath no interest; nor even
with the feigned interest of a man that would move the
passions of others, when he feeleth no emotion himself;
but with joy and gladness, such as angels only can know.
They sang the story out, for they could not stay to tell it in
heavy prose. They sang, "Glory to God on high, and on
earth peace, good will towards men." Methinks they sang
it with gladness in their eyes; with their hearts burning
with love, and with breasts as full of joy as if the good news
to man had been good news to themselves. And, verily, it
was good news to them, for the heart of sympathy makes
good news to others, good news to itself. Do you not love
the angels? Ye will not bow before them, and there ye are
right; but will ye not love them? Doth it not make one part
of your anticipation of heaven, that in heaven you shall
dwell with the holy angels, as well as with the spirits of
the just made perfect? Oh, how sweet to think that these
holy and lovely beings are our guardians every hour! They
keep watch and ward about us, both in the burning noon-
tide, and in the darkness of the night. They keep us in all
our ways; they bear us up in their hands, lest at any time
we dash our feet against stones. They unceasingly minister unto us who are the heirs of salvation; both by day and
night they are our watchers and our guardians, for know
ye not, that "the angel of the Lord encampeth round about
them that fear him."

Let us turn aside, having just thought of angels for a
moment, to think rather of this song, than of the angels
themselves. Their song was brief, but as Kitto excellent-
ly remarks, it was "well worthy of angels expressing the
greatest and most blessed truths, in words so few, that
they become to an acute apprehension, almost oppressive
by the pregnant fulness of their meaning" — "Glory to God
in the highest, on earth peace, good will toward men." We
shall, hoping to be assisted by the Holy Spirit, look at these
words of the angels in a fourfold manner. I shall just suggest some instructive thoughts arising from these words;
then some emotional thoughts; then a few prophetical
thoughts; and afterwards, one or two preceptive thoughts.

I. First then, in the words of our text. There are many
instructive thoughts. The angels sang something which

men could understand—something which men ought to understand—something which will make men much better if they will understand it. The angels were singing about Jesus who was born in the manger. We must look upon their song as being built upon this foundation. They sang of Christ, and the salvation which he came into this world to work out. And what they said of this salvation was this: they said, first, that it gave glory to God; secondly, that it gave peace to man; and, thirdly, that it was a token of God's good will towards the human race.

1. First, they said that this salvation gave glory to God. They had been present on many august occasions, and they had joined in many a solemn chorus to the praise of their almighty creator. They were present at the creation: "The morning stars sang together, and all the sons of God shouted for joy." They had seen many a planet fashioned between the palms of Jehovah, and wheeled by his eternal hands through the infinitude of space. They had sung solemn songs over many a world which the great One had created. We doubt not, they had often chanted "Blessing and honour, and glory, and majesty, and power, and dominion, and might, be unto him that sitteth on the throne," manifesting himself in the work of creation. I doubt not, too, that their songs had gathered force through ages. As when first created, their first breath was song, so when they saw God create new worlds then their song received another note; they rose a little higher in the gamut of adoration. But this time, when they saw God stoop from his throne, and become a babe, hanging upon a woman's breast, they lifted their notes higher still; and reaching to the uttermost stretch of angelic music, they gained the highest notes of the divine scale of praise, and they sung, "Glory to God in the highest," for higher in goodness they felt God could not go. Thus their highest praise they gave to him in the highest act of his godhead. If it be true that there is a hierarchy of angels, rising tier upon tier in magnificence and dignity—if the apostle teaches us that there be "angels, and principalities, and powers, and thrones, and dominions," amongst these blest inhabitants of the upper world—I can suppose that when the intelligence was first communicated to those angels that are to be found upon the outskirts of the heavenly world, when they looked down from heaven and saw the newborn babe, they sent the news backward to the place whence the miracle first proceeded, singing

"Angels, from the realms of glory,
  Wing your downward flight to earth,
  Ye who sing creation's story,
  Now proclaim Messiah's birth;
  Come and worship,
  Worship Christ, the newborn King."

And as the message ran from rank to rank, at last the presence angels, those four cherubim that perpetually watch around the throne of God—those wheels with eyes—took up the strain, and, gathering up the song of all the inferior grades of angels, surmounted the divine pinnacle of harmony with their own solemn chant of adoration, upon which the entire host shouted, "The highest angels praise thee."—"Glory to God in the highest." Ay, there is no mortal that can ever dream how magnificent was that song. Then, note, if angels shouted before and when the world was made, their hallelujahs were more full, more strong, more magnificent, if not more hearty, when they saw Jesus Christ born of the Virgin Mary to be man's redeemer—"Glory to God in the highest."

What is the instructive lesson to be learned from this first syllable of the angels' song? Why this, that salvation is God's highest glory. He is glorified in every dew drop that twinkles to the morning sun. He is magnified in every wood flower that blossoms in the copse, although it live to blush unseen, and waste its sweetness in the forest air. God is glorified in every bird that warbles on the spray; in every lamb that skips the mead. Do not the fishes in the sea praise him? From the tiny minnow to the huge Leviathan, do not all creatures that swim the water bless and praise his name? Do not all created things extol him? Is there aught beneath the sky, save man, that doth not glorify God? Do not the stars exalt him, when they write his name upon the azure of heaven in their golden letters? Do not the lightnings adore him when they flash his brightness in arrows of light piercing the midnight darkness? Do not thunders extol him when they roll like drums in the march of the God of armies? Do not all things exalt him, from the least even to the greatest? But sing, sing, oh universe, till thou hast exhausted thyself, thou canst not afford a song so sweet as the song of incarnation. Though creation may be a majestic organ of praise, it cannot reach the compass of the golden canticle—incarnation. There is more in that than in creation, more melody in Jesus in the manger, than there is in worlds on worlds rolling their grandeur round the throne of the Most High. Pause Christian, and consider this a minute. See how every attribute is here magnified. Lo! what wisdom is here. God becomes man that God may be just, and the justifier of the ungodly. Lo, what power, for where is power so great as when it concealeth power? What power, that Godhead should unrobe itself and become man. Behold, what love is thus revealed to us when Jesus becomes a man. Behold ye, what faithfulness. How many promises are this day kept? How many solemn obligations are this hour discharged? Tell me one attribute of God that is not manifest in Jesus; and your ignorance shall be the reason why you have not seen it so. The whole of God is glorified in Christ; and though some part of the name of God is written in the universe, it is here best read—in Him who was the Son of Man, and, yet, the Son of God.

But, let me say one word here before I go away from this point. We must learn from this, that if salvation glorifies God, glorifies him in the highest degree, and makes the highest creatures praise him, this one reflection may be added—then, that doctrine, which glorifies man in salvation cannot be the gospel. For salvation glorifies God. The angels were no Arminians, they sang, "Glory to God in the highest." They believe in no doctrine which uncrowns Christ, and puts the crown upon the head of mortals. They believe in no system of faith which makes salvation dependent upon the creature, and, which really gives the creature the praise, for what is it less than for a man to save himself, if the whole dependence of salvation rests upon his own free will? No, my brethren; they may be some preachers, that delight to preach a doctrine that magnifies man; but in their gospel angels have no delight. The only glad tidings that made the angels sing, are those that put God first, God last, God midst, and God without end, in the salvation of his creatures, and put the crown wholly and alone upon the head of him that saves without a helper. "Glory to God in the highest," is the angels' song.

2. When they had sung this, they sang what they had never sung before. "Glory to God in the highest," was an old, old song; they had sung that from before the foundations of the world. But, now, they sang as it were a new song before the throne of God for they added this stanza—"on earth, peace." They did not sing that in the garden. There was peace there, but it seemed a thing of course, and scarce worth singing of. There was more than peace there;

for there was glory to God there. But, now, man had fallen, and since the day when cherubim with fiery swords drove out the man, there had been no peace on earth, save in the breast of some believers, who had obtained peace from the living fountain of this incarnation of Christ. Wars had raged from the ends of the world; men had slaughtered one another, heaps on heaps. There had been wars within as well as wars without. Conscience had fought with man; Satan had tormented man with thoughts of sin. There had been no peace on earth since Adam fell. But, now, when the newborn King made his appearance, the swaddling band with which he was wrapped up was the white flag of peace. That manger was the place where the treaty was signed, whereby warfare should be stopped between man's conscience and himself, man's conscience and his God. It was then, that day, the trumpet blew — "Sheathe the sword, oh man, sheathe the sword, oh conscience, for God is now at peace with man, and man at peace with God." Do you not feel my brethren, that the gospel of God is peace to man? Where else can peace be found, but in the message of Jesus? Go legalist, work for peace with toil and pain, and thou shalt never find it. Go, thou, that trustest in the law, go thou, to Sinai; look to the flames that Moses saw, and shrink, and tremble, and despair; for peace is nowhere to be found, but in him, of whom it is said, "This man shall be peace." And what a peace it is, beloved! It is peace like a river, and righteousness like the waves of the sea. It is the peace of God that passeth all understanding, which keeps our hearts and minds through Jesus Christ our Lord. This sacred peace between the pardoned soul and God the pardoner; this marvelous at-one-ment between the sinner and his judge, this was it that the angels sung when they said, "peace on earth."

3. And, then, they wisely ended their song with a third note. They said, "Good will to man." Philosophers have said that God has a good will toward man; but I never knew any man who derived much comfort from their philosophical assertion. Wise men have thought from what we have seen in creation that God had much good will toward man, or else his works would never have been so constructed for their comfort; but I never heard of any man who could risk his soul's peace upon such a faint hope as that. But I have not only heard of thousands, but I know them, who are quite sure that God has a good will towards men; and if you ask their reason, they will give a full and

perfect answer. They say, he has good will toward man for he gave his Son. No greater proof of kindness between the Creator and his subjects can possibly be afforded than when the Creator gives his only begotten and well beloved Son to die. Though the first note is God-like, and though the second note is peaceful, this third note melts my heart the most. Some think of God as if he were a morose being who hated all mankind. Some picture him as if he were some abstract subsistence taking no interest in our affairs. Hark ye, God has "good will toward men." You know what good will means. Well, swearer, you have cursed God; he has not fulfilled his curse on you; he has good will towards you, though you have no good will towards him. Infidel, you have sinned high and hard against the Most High; he has said no hard things against you, for he has good will towards men. Poor sinner, thou hast broken his laws; thou art half afraid to come to the throne of his mercy lest he should spurn thee; hear thou this, and be comforted—God has good will towards men, so good a will that he has said, and said it with an oath too, "As I live, saith the Lord, I have no pleasure in the death of him that dieth, but had rather that he should turn unto me and live;" so good a will moreover that he has even condescended to say, "Come, now, let us reason together; though your sins be as scarlet, they shall be as wool; though they be red like crimson, they shall be whiter than snow." And if you say, "Lord, how shall I know that thou hast this good will towards me," he points to yonder manger, and says, "Sinner, if I had not a good will towards thee, would I have parted with my Son? If I had not good will towards the human race, would I have given up my Son to become one of that race that he might by so doing redeem them from death?" Ye that doubt the Master's love, look ye to that circle of angels; see their blaze of glory; hear their son, and let your doubts die away in that sweet music and be buried in a shroud of harmony. He has good will to men; he is willing to pardon; he passes by iniquity, transgression, and sin. And mark thee, if Satan shall then add, "But though God hath good will, yet he cannot violate his justice, therefore his mercy may be ineffective, and you may die;" then listen to that first note of the song, "Glory to God in the highest," and reply to Satan and all his temptations, that when God shows good will to a penitent sinner, there is not only peace in the sinner's heart, but it brings glory to every attribute of God, and so he can be just, and yet justify the sinner, and glorify himself.

I do not pretend to say that I have opened all the instructions contained in these three sentences, but I may perhaps direct you into a train of thought that may serve you for the week. I hope that all through the week you will have a truly merry Christmas by feeling the power of these words, and knowing the unction of them. "Glory to God in the highest, on earth peace, good will toward men."

II. Next, I have to present to you some emotional thoughts. Friends, doth not this verse, this song of angels, stir your heart with happiness? When I read that, and found the angels singing it, I thought to myself, "Then if the angels ushered in the gospel's great head with singing, ought I not to preach with singing? And ought not my hearers to live with singing? Ought not their hearts to be glad and their spirits to rejoice?" Well, thought I, there be some somber religionists who were born in a dark night in December that think a smile upon the face is wicked, and believe that for a Christian to be glad and rejoice is to be inconsistent. Ah, I wish these gentlemen had seen the angels when they sang about Christ; for angels sang about his birth, though it was no concern of theirs, certainly men ought to sing about it as long as they live, sing about it when they die, and sing about it when they live in heaven for ever. I do long to see in the midst of the church more of a singing Christianity. The last few years have been breeding in our midst a groaning and unbelieving Christianity. Now, I doubt not its sincerity, but I do doubt its healthy character. I say it may be true and real enough; God forbid I should say a word against the sincerity of those who practice it; but it is a sickly religion. Watts hit the mark when he said,

"Religion never was designed
To make our pleasures less."

It is designed to do away with some of our pleasures, but it gives us many more, to make up for what it takes away; so it does not make them less. O ye that see in Christ nothing but a subject to stimulate your doubts and make the tears run down your cheeks; O ye that always say,

"Lord, what a wretched land is this,
That yields us no supplies,"

Come ye hither and see the angels. Do they tell their sto-

ry with groans, and sobs, and sighs? Ah, no; they shout
aloud, "Glory to God in the highest." Now, imitate them,
my dear brethren. If you are professors of religion, try always to have a cheerful carriage. Let others mourn; but

> "Why should the children of a king
>   Go mourning all their days?"

Anoint your head and wash your face; appear not unto
men to fast. Rejoice in the Lord always, and again I say
unto you rejoice. Specially this week be not ashamed to
be glad. You need not think it a wicked thing to be happy.
Penance and whipping, and misery are no such very vir-
tuous things, after all. The damned are miserable; let the
saved be happy. Why should you hold fellowship with the
lost by feelings of perpetual mourning? Why not rather
anticipate the joys of heaven, and begin to sing on earth
that song which you will never need to end? The first emotion then that we ought to cherish in our hearts is the emotion of joy and gladness.

Well, what next? Another emotion is that of confidence.
I am not sure that I am right in calling that an emotion, but
still in me it is so much akin to it, that I will venture to be
wrong if I be so. Now, if when Christ came on this earth
God had sent some black creature down from heaven, (if
there be such creatures there) to tell us, "Glory to God in
the highest, and on earth peace, good will toward men,"
and if with a frowning brow and a stammering tongue he
delivered his message, if I had been there and heard it,
I should have scrupled to believe him, for I should have
said, "You don't look like the messenger that God would
send—stammering fellow as you are—with such glad
news as this." But when the angels came there was no
doubting the truth of what they said, because it was quite
certain that the angels believed it; they told it as if they did,
for they told it with singing, with joy and gladness. If some
friend, having heard that a legacy was left you, and should
come to you with a solemn countenance, and a tongue
like a funeral bell, saying, "Do you know so-and-so has
left you £10,000!" Why you would say, "Ah! I dare say,"
and laugh in his face. But if your brother should suddenly
burst into your room, and exclaim, "I say, what do you
think? You are a rich man; So-and-so has left you £10,000!"
Why you would say, "I think it is very likely to be true, for
he looks so happy over it." Well, when these angels came
from heaven they told the news just as if they believed

it; and though I have often wickedly doubted my Lord's good will, I think I never could have doubted it while I heard those angels singing. No, I should say, "The messengers themselves are proof of the truth, for it seems they have heard it from God's lips; they have no doubt about it, for see how joyously they tell the news." Now, poor soul, thou that art afraid lest God should destroy thee, and thou thinkest that God will never have mercy upon thee, look at the singing angels and doubt if thou darest. Do not go to the synagogue of long-faced hypocrites to hear the minister who preaches with a nasal twang, with misery in his face, whilst he tells you that God has good will towards men; I know you won't believe what he says, for he does not preach with joy in his countenance; he is telling you good news with a grunt, and you are not likely to receive it. But go straightway to the plain where Bethlehem shepherds sat by night, and when you hear the angels singing out the gospel, by the grace of God upon you, you cannot help believing that they manifestly feel the preciousness of telling. Blessed Christmas, that brings such creatures as angels to confirm our faith in God's good will to men!

III. I must now bring before you the third point. There are some prophetic utterances contained in these words. The angels sang "Glory to God in the highest, on earth peace, good will toward men." But I look around, and what see I in the wide, wide world? I do not see God honored. I see the heathen bowing down before their idols; I mark the Romanist casting himself before the rotten rags of his relics, and the ugly figures of his images. I look about me, and I see tyranny lording it over the bodies and souls of men; I see God forgotten; I see a worldly race pursuing mammon; I see a bloody race pursuing Moloch; I see ambition riding like Nimrod over the land, God forgotten, his name dishonored. And was this all the angels sang about? Is this all that made them sing "Glory to God in the highest?" Ah! no. There are brighter days approaching. They sang, "Peace on earth." But I hear still the clarion of war; and the cannon's horrid roar; not yet have they turned the sword into a ploughshare, and the spear into a pruning-hook. War still reigns. Is this all that the angels sang about? And whilst I see wars to the ends of the earth, am I to believe that this was all the angels expected? Ah! no, brethren; the angels' song is big with prophecy; it travaileth in birth with glories. A few more years, and he that lives them out shall see why angels sang; a few more years, and he that will come shall come, and will not tarry. Christ the Lord will come again, and when he cometh he shall cast the idols from their thrones; he shall dash down every fashion of heresy and every shape of idolatry; he shall reign from pole to pole with illimitable sway; he shall reign, when like a scroll, yon blue heavens have passed away. No strife shall vex Messiah's reign, no blood shall then be shed; they'll hang the useless helmet high, and study war no more. The hour is approaching when the temple of Janus shall be shut for ever, and when cruel Mars shall be hooted from the earth. The day is coming when the lion shall eat straw like the ox, when the leopard shall lie down with the kid; when the weaned child shall put his hand upon the cockatrice den and play with the asp. The hour approacheth; the first streaks of the sunlight have made glad the age in which we live. Lo, he comes, with trumpets and with clouds of glory; he shall come for whom we look with joyous expectation, whose coming shall be glory to his redeemed, and confusion to his enemies. Ah, brethren, when the angels sang this there was an echo through the long aisles of a glorious future. That echo was—

"Hallelujah! Christ the Lord
God Omnipotent shall reign."

Ay, and doubtless the angels heard by faith the fulness of the song,

"Hark! the song of jubilee
Loud as mighty thunders' roar,
Or the fulness of the sea,
When it breaks upon the shore."

"Christ the Lord Omnipotent reigneth."

IV. Now, I have one more lesson for you, and I have done. That lesson is preceptive. I wish everybody that keeps Christmas this year, would keep it as the angels kept it. There are many persons who, when they talk about keeping Christmas, mean by that the cutting of the bands of their religion for one day in the year, as if Christ were the Lord of misrule, as if the birth of Christ should be celebrated like the orgies of Bacchus. There are some very religious people, that on Christmas would never forget to go to church in the morning; they believe Christmas to be nearly as holy as Sunday, for they reverence the tradition of the elders. Yet their way of spending the rest of the day is very remarkable; for if they see their way straight up stairs to their bed at night, it must be by accident. They would not consider they had kept Christmas in a proper manner, if they did not verge on gluttony and drunkenness. They are many who think Christmas cannot possibly be kept, except there be a great shout of merriment and mirth in the house, and added to that the boisterousness of sin. Now, my brethren, although we, as successors of the Puritans, will not keep the day in any religious sense whatever, attaching nothing more to it than to any other day: believing that every day may be a Christmas for ought we know, and wishing to make every day Christmas, if we can, yet we must try to set an example to others how to behave on that day; and especially since the angels gave glory to God: let us do the same.

Once more the angels said, "Peace to men:" let us labor if we can to make peace next Christmas day. Now, old gentleman, you won't take your son in; he has offended you. Fetch him at Christmas. "Peace on earth;" you know: that is a Christmas Carol. Make peace in your family.

Now, brother, you have made a vow that you will never speak to your brother again. Go after him and say, "Oh, my dear fellow, let not this day's sun go down upon our wrath." Fetch him in, and give him your hand. Now, Mr. Tradesman, you have an opponent in trade, and you have said some very hard words about him lately. If you do not make the matter up today, or tomorrow, or as soon as you can, yet do it on that day. That is the way to keep Christmas, peace on earth and glory to God. And oh, if thou hast anything on thy conscience, anything that prevents thy having peace of mind, keep thy Christmas in thy chamber, praying to God to give thee peace; for it is peace on earth, mind, peace in thyself, peace with thyself, peace with thy fellow men, peace with thy God. And do not think thou hast well celebrated that day till thou canst say, "O God,

'With the world, myself, and thee
I ere I sleep at peace will be. "

And when the Lord Jesus has become your peace, remember, there is another thing, good will towards men. Do not try to keep Christmas without keeping good will towards men. You are a gentleman, and have servants. Well, try and set their chimneys on fire with a large piece of good, substantial beef for them. If you are men of wealth, you have poor in your neighborhood. Find something wherewith to clothe the naked, and feed the hungry, and make glad the mourner. Remember, it is good will towards men. Try, if you can, to show them good will at this special season; and if you will do that, the poor will say with me, that indeed they wish there were six Christmases in the year.

Let each one of us go from this place determined, that if we are angry all the year round, this next week shall be an exception; that if we have snarled at everybody last year, this Christmas time we will strive to be kindly affectionate to others; and if we have lived all this year at enmity with God, I pray that by his Spirit he may this week give us peace with him; and then, indeed, my brother, it will be the merriest Christmas we ever had in all our lives. You are going home to your father and mother, young men; many of you are going from your shops to your homes. You remember what I preached on last Christmas time. Go home to thy friends, and tell them what the Lord hath done for thy soul, and that will make a blessed round of stories at the Christmas fire. If you will each of you tell your parents how the Lord met with you in the house of prayer; how, when you left home, you were a gay, wild blade, but have now come back to love your mother's God, and read your father's Bible. Oh, what a happy Christmas that will make! What more shall I say? May God give you peace with yourselves; may he give you good will towards all your friends, your enemies, and your neighbors; and may he give you grace to give glory to God in the highest. I will say no more, except at the close of this sermon to wish every one of you, when the day shall come, the happiest Christmas you ever had in your lives.

"Now with angels round the throne,
Cherubim and seraphim,
And the church, which still is one,
Let us swell the solemn hymn;
Glory to the great I AM!
Glory to the Victim Lamb.

Blessing, honour, glory, might,
And dominion infinite,
To the Father of our Lord,
To the Spirit and the Word;
As it was all worlds before,
Is, and shall be evermore."

VI. THE INCARNATION AND BIRTH OF CHRIST

"But thou, Bethlehem Ephratah, though thou be little among the thousands of Judah, yet out of thee shall he come forth unto me that is to be ruler in Israel; whose goings forth have been from of old, from everlasting."
Micah 5:2

This is the season of the year when, whether we wish it or not, we are compelled to think of the birth of Christ. I hold it to be one of the greatest absurdities under heaven to think that there is any religion in keeping Christmas day. There are no probabilities whatever that our Saviour Jesus Christ was born on that day, and the observance of it is purely of Popish origin; doubtless those who are Catholics have a right to hallow it, but I do not see how consistent Protestants can account it in the least sacred. However, I wish there were ten or a dozen Christmas days in the year; for there is work enough in the world, and a little more rest would not hurt labouring people. Christmas day is really a boon to us; particularly as it enables us to assemble round the family hearth and meet our friends once more. Still, although we do not fall exactly in the track of other people, I see no harm in thinking of the incarnation and birth of the Lord Jesus. We do not wish to be classed with those—

"Who with more care keep holiday
The wrong, than others the right way."

The old Puritans made a parade of work on Christmas day, just to show that they protested against the observance of it. But we believe they entered that protest so completely, that we are willing, as their descendants, to take the good accidentally conferred by the day, and leave its superstitions to the superstitious.

To proceed at once to what we have to say to you we notice, first, who it was that sent Christ forth. God the

Father here speaks, and says, "Out of thee shall he come
forth unto me that is to be the ruler in Israel." Secondly,
where did he come to at the time of his incarnation? Thirdly, what did he come for? "To be ruler in Israel." Fourth-
ly, had he ever come before? Yes, he had. "Whose goings
forth have been from of old, from everlasting."

I. First, then, who sent Jesus Christ? The answer is returned to us by the words of the text. "Out of thee" saith
Jehovah, speaking by the mouth of Micah, "Out of thee
shall he come forth unto me." It is a sweet thought that Jesus Christ, did not come forth without his Father's permis-
sion, authority, consent, and assistance. He was sent of the
Father, that he might be the saviour of men. We are, alas!
too apt to forget, that while there are distinctions as to the
persons in the Trinity, there are no distinctions of honor;
and we do very frequently ascribe the honor of our salvation, or at least the depths of its mercy and the extremity
of its benevolence, more to Jesus Christ than we do to the
Father. This is a very great mistake. What if Jesus came?
Did not his Father send him? If he was made a child did
not the Holy Ghost beget him? If he spake wondrously,
did not his Father pour grace into his lips, that he might
be an able minister of the new covenant? If his Father did
forsake him when he drank the bitter cup of gall, did he
not love him still? And did he not, by and by, after three
days, raise him from the dead, and at last receive him up
on high, leading captivity captive? Ah, beloved, he who
knoweth the Father, and the Son, and the Holy Ghost as
he should know them, never setteth one before another;
he is not more thankful to one than the other; he sees them
at Bethlehem, at Gethsemane, and on Calvary, all equal-
ly engaged in the work of salvation. "He shall come forth
unto me." O Christian, hast thou put thy confidence in
the man Christ Jesus? Hast thou placed thy reliance solely
on him? And art thou united with him? Then believe that
thou art united unto the God of heaven; since to the man
Christ Jesus thou art brother and holdest closest fellowship, thou art linked thereby with God the Eternal, and
"the Ancient of days" is thy Father and thy friend. "He
shall come forth unto me". Did you never see the depth
of love there was in the heart of Jehovah, when God the
Father equipped his Son for the great enterprise of mercy?
There had been a sad day in Heaven once before, when
Satan fell, and dragged with him a third of the stars of
heaven, and when the Son of God launching from his great

right hand the Omnipotent thunders, dashed the rebellious crew to the pit of perdition; but if we could conceive
a grief in heaven, that must have been a sadder day, when
the Son of the Most High left his Father's bosom, where
he had lain from before all worlds "Go," saith the Father,
"and thy Father's blessing on thy head!" Then comes the
unrobing. How do angels crowd around to see the Son of
God take off his robes. He laid aside his crown; he said,
"My father, I am Lord over all, blessed for ever, but I will
lay my crown aside, and be as mortal men are." He strips
himself of his bright vest of glory; "Father," he says, "I
will wear a robe of clay, just such a men wear." Then he
takes off all those jewels wherewith he was glorified; he
lays aside his starry mantles and robes of light, to dress
himself in the simple garments of the peasant of Galilee.
What a solemn disrobing that must have been! And next,
can you picture the dismissal! The angels attend the Saviour through the streets, until they approach the doors:
when an angel cries, "Lift up your heads, O ye gates, and
be ye lifted up ye everlasting doors, and let the king of
glory through!" Oh! methinks the angels must have wept
when they lost the company of Jesus—when the sun of
heaven bereaved them of all its light. But they went after
him. They descended with him; and when his spirit entered into flesh and he became a babe, he was attended by
that mighty host of angels, who after they had been with
him to Bethlehem's manger, and seen him safely, laid on
his mother's breast, in their journey upwards appeared to
the shepherds and told them that he was born king of the
Jews. The Father sent him! Contemplate that subject. Let
your soul get hold of it, and in every period of his life think
that he suffered what the Father willed; that every step of
his life was marked with the approval of the great I AM.
Let every thought that you have of Jesus be also connected
with the eternal, ever-blessed God; for "he," saith Jehovah,
"shall come forth unto me." Who sent him, then? The answer is, his Father.

II. Now, secondly, where did he come to? A word or
two concerning Bethlehem. It seemed meet and right that
our saviour should be born in Bethlehem and that because
of Bethlehem's history, Bethlehem's name, and Bethlehem's position—little in Judah.

1. First, it seemed necessary that Christ should be born
in Bethlehem, because of Bethlehem's history. Dear to every Israelite was the little village of Bethlehem. Jerusalem

might outshine it in splendour; for there stood the temple, the glory of the whole earth, and "beautiful for situation, the joy of the whole earth was Mount Zion;" yet around Bethlehem there clustered a number of incidents which always made it a pleasant resting-place to every Jewish mind; and even the Christian cannot help loving Bethlehem. The first mention, I think, that we have of Bethlehem is a sorrowful one. There Rachel died. If you turn to the 35th of Genesis you will find it said in the 16th verse—

> "And they journeyed from Bethel; and there was but a little way to come to Ephrath; and Rachel travailed, and she had hard labour. And it came to pass, when she was in hard labour, that the midwife said unto her, Fear not; thou shalt have this son also. And it came to pass, as her soul was in departing, (for she died) that she called his name Ben-oni: but his father called him Benjamin. And Rachel died, and was buried in the way to Ephrath, which is Bethlehem. And Jacob set a pillar upon her grave, that is the pillar of Rachel's grave unto this day."

A singular incident this—almost prophetic. Might not Mary have called her own son Jesus, her Ben-oni; for he was to be the child of Sorrow? Simeon said to her—

> "Yea, a sword shall pierce through thine own soul also, that the thoughts of many hearts may be revealed."

But while she might have called him Ben-oni, what did God his Father call him? Benjamin, the son of my right hand. Ben-oni was he as a man; Benjamin as to his Godhead. This little incident seems to be almost a prophecy that Ben-oni—Benjamin, the Lord Jesus, should be born in Bethlehem.

But another woman makes this place celebrated. That woman's name was Naomi. There lived at Bethlehem in after days, when, perhaps, the stone that Jacob's fondness had raised had been covered with moss and its inscription obliterated, another woman named Naomi. She too was a daughter of joy, and yet a daughter of bitterness. Naomi was a woman whom the Lord had loved and blessed, but she had to go to a strange land; and she said, "Call me not Naomi (pleasant) but let my name be called Mara (bitter) for the Almighty hath dealt very bitterly with me." Yet was she not alone amid all her losses, for there cleaved unto her Ruth the Moabitess, whose Gentile blood should unite with the pure untainted stream of the Jew, and should

thus bring forth the Lord our Saviour, the great king both
of Jews and Gentiles. That very beautiful book of Ruth had
all its scenery laid in Bethlehem. It was at Bethlehem that
Ruth went forth to glean in the fields of Boaz; it was there
that Boaz looked upon her, and she bowed herself before
her lord; it was there her marriage was celebrated; and in
the streets of Bethlehem did Boaz and Ruth receive a blessing which made them fruitful so that Boaz became the father of Obed, and Obed the father of Jesse, and Jesse the
father of David. That last fact gilds Bethlehem with glory—the fact that David was born there—the mighty hero
who smote the Philistine giant, who led the discontented
of his land away from the tyranny of their monarch, and
who afterwards, by a full consent of a willing people, was
crowned king of Israel and Judah. Bethlehem was a royal city, because the kings were there brought forth. Little
as Bethlehem was, it was much to be esteemed; because it
was like certain principalities which we have in Europe,
which are celebrated for nothing but for bringing forth
the consorts of the royal families of England. It was right,
then, from history, that Bethlehem should be the birthplace of Christ.

2. But again, there is something in the name of the
place. "Bethlehem Ephratah." The word Bethlehem has
a double meaning. It signifies "the house of bread," and
"the house of war." Ought not Jesus Christ to be born in
"the house of bread?" He is the bread of his people, on
which they feed. As our fathers ate manna in the wilderness, so do we live on Jesus here below. Famished by the
world, we cannot feed on its shadows. Its husks may grat-
ify the swinish taste of worldlings, for they are swine; but
we need something more substantial, and in that blest
bread of heaven, made of the bruised body of our Lord
Jesus, and baked in the furnace of his agonies, we find a
blessed food. No food like Jesus to the desponding soul
or to the strongest saint. The very meanest of the family
of God goes to Bethlehem for his bread; and the strongest man, who eats strong meat, goes to Bethlehem for it.
House of Bread! whence could come our nourishment but
from thee? We have tried Sinai, but on her rugged steeps
there grow no fruits, and her thorny heights yield no corn
whereon we may feed. We have repaired even to Tabor
itself, where Christ was transfigured, and yet there we
have not been able to eat his flesh and drink his blood. But
Bethlehem, thou house of bread, rightly wast thou called;

for there the bread of life was first handed down for man
to eat. And it is also called "the house of war;" because
Christ is to a man "the house of bread," or else "the house
of war." While he is food to the righteous he causeth war
to the wicked, according to his own word—

> "Think not that I am come to send peace on the earth; I am not
> come to send peace, but a sword. For I am come to set a man
> at variance against his father, and the daughter against her
> mother, and the daughter-in-law against her mother-in-law.
> And a man's foes shall be they of his own household."

Sinner! if thou dost not know Bethlehem as "the house of
bread," it shall be to thee a "house of war." If from the lips
of Jesus thou dost never drink sweet honey—if thou art
not like the bee, which sippeth sweet luscious liquor from
the rose of Sharon, then out of the selfsame mouth there
shall go forth against thee a two-edged sword; and that
mouth from which the righteous draw their bread, shall be
to thee the mouth of destruction and the cause of thine ill.
Jesus of Bethlehem, house of bread and house of war, we
trust we know thee as our bread. Oh! that some who are
now at war with thee might hear in their hearts, as well as
in their ears the song—

> "Peace on earth, and mercy mild.
> God and sinners reconciled."

And now for that word Ephratah. That was the old
name of the place which the Jews retained and loved. The
meaning of it is, "fruitfulness," or "abundance." Ah, well
was Jesus born in the house of fruitfulness; for whence
cometh my fruitfulness and any fruitfulness, my brother,
but from Bethlehem? Our poor barren hearts ne'er pro-
duced one fruit, or flower, till they were watered with the
saviour's blood. It is his incarnation which fattens the soil
of our hearts. There had been pricking thorns on all the
ground, and mortal poisons, before be came; but our fruitfulness comes from him. "I am like a green fir-tree; from
thee is my fruit found." "All my springs are in thee." If we
be like trees planted by the rivers of water, bringing forth
our fruit in our season, it is not because we were naturally fruitful, but because of the rivers of water by which
we were planted. It is Jesus that makes us fruitful. "If a
man abide in me," he says, "and my words abide him, he
shall bring forth much fruit." Glorious Bethlehem Ephra-

tah! Rightly named! Fruitful house of bread — the house of abundant provision for the people of God!

3. We notice, next, the position of Bethlehem. It is said to be "little among the thousands of Judah." Why is this? Because Jesus Christ always goes among little ones. He was born in the little one "among the thousands of Judah." No Bashan's high hill, not on Hebron's royal mount, not in Jerusalem's palaces, but the humble, yet illustrious, village of Bethlehem. There is a passage in Zechariah which teaches us a lesson, it is said that the man on the red horse stood among the myrtle-trees. Now the myrtle-trees grow at the bottom of the hill; and the man on the red horse always rides there. He does not ride on the mountain-top; he rides among the humble in heart. "With this man will I dwell, saith the Lord, with him who is of a humble and contrite spirit, and who trembleth at my word." There are some little ones here this morning — "little among the thousands of Judah." No one ever heard your name, did they? If you were buried, and had your name on your tombstone, it would never be noticed. Those who pass by would say, "it is nothing to me, I never knew him." You do not know much of yourself, or think much of yourself; you can scarcely read, perhaps. Or if you have some talent and ability, you are despised amongst men; or, if you are not despised by them, you despise yourself. You are one of the little ones. Well, Christ is always born in Bethlehem among the little ones. Big hearts never get Christ inside of them; Christ lieth not in great hearts, but in little ones. Mighty and proud spirits never have Jesus Christ, for he cometh in at low doors, but he will not come in at high ones. He who hath a broken heart, and a low spirit, shall have the saviour, but none else. He healeth not the prince and the king, but "the broken in heart, and he bindeth up their wounds." Sweet thought! He is the Christ of the little ones. "Thou, Bethlehem Ephratah, though thou be little among the thousands of Judah yet out of thee shall he come forth unto me that is to be ruler in Israel."

We cannot pass away from this without another thought here, which is, how wonderfully mysterious was that providence which brought Jesus Christ's mother to Bethlehem at the very time when she was to be delivered! His parents were residing at Nazareth, and what should they want to travel at that time for? Naturally, they would have remained at home, it was not at all likely that his mother would have taken journey to Bethlehem while in so peculiar a condition, but Caesar Augustus issues a decree that they are to be taxed. Very well, then, let them be taxed at Nazareth. No, it pleases him that they should all go to their city. But why should Caesar Augustus think of it just at that particular time? Simply because, while man deviseth his way, the king's heart is in the hand of the Lord. Why, what a thousand chances, as the world has it, met together to bring about this event! First of all, Caesar quarrels with Herod; one of the Herods was deposed; Caesar says, "I shall tax Judea, and make it a province, instead of having it for a separate kingdom." Well, it must be done. But when is it to be done? This taxing, it is said, was first commenced when Cyreneus was governor. But why is the census to be taken at that particular period—suppose, December? Why not have had it last October and why could not the people be taxed where they were living? Was not their money just as good there as anywhere else? It was Caesar's whim; but it was God's decree. Oh, we love the sublime doctrine of eternal absolute predestination. Some have doubted its being consistent with the free agency of man. We know well it is so, and we never saw any difficulty in the subject; we believe metaphysicians have made difficulties; we see none ourselves. It is for us to believe, that man does as he pleases, yet notwithstanding he always does as God decrees. If Judas betrays Christ, "thereunto he was appointed;" and if Pharaoh hardens his heart, yet, "for this purpose have I raised thee up, for to show forth my power in thee." Man doth as he wills; but God maketh him do as he willeth, too. Nay, not only is the will of man under the absolute predestination of Jehovah; but all things, great or little, are of him. Well hath the good poet said, "Doubtless the sailing of a cloud hath Providence to its pilot; doubtless the root of an oak is gnarled for a special purpose, God compasseth all things, mantling the globe like air." There is nothing great or little, that is not from him. The summer dust moves in its orbit, guided by the same hand which rolls the stars along; the dewdrops have their father, and trickle on the rose leaf as God bids them; yea, the sear leaves of the forest, when hurled along by the tempest, have their allotted position where they shall fall, nor can they go beyond it. In the great, and in the little, there is God—God in everything, working all things according to the counsel of his own will; and though man seeks to go against his Maker, yet he cannot. God hath bounded the sea with a barrier of sand; and if the sea mount up wave after wave, yet it shall not exceed its allotted channel. Everything is of God and unto him who guideth the stars and wingeth sparrows, who ruleth planets and yet moveth atoms, who speaks thunders and yet whispers zephyrs, unto him be glory; for there is God in everything.

III. This brings us to the third point: what did Jesus come for? He came to be "ruler in Israel." A very singular thing is this, that Jesus Christ was said to have been "born the king of the Jews." Very few have ever been "born king." Men are born princes, but they are seldom born kings. I do not think you can find an instance in history where any infant was born king. He was the prince of Wales, perhaps, and he had to wait a number of years, till his father died, and then they manufactured him into a king, by putting a crown on his head; and a sacred chrism, and other silly things; but he was not born a king. I remember no one who was born a king except Jesus; and there is emphatic meaning in that verse that we sing

"Born thy people to deliver;
  Born a child, and yet a king."

The moment that he came on earth he was a king. He did not wait till his majority that he might take his empire; but as soon as his eye greeted the sunshine he was a king; from the moment that his little hands grasped anything, they grasped a sceptre, as soon as his pulse beat, and his blood began to flow, his heart beat royally, and his pulse beat an imperial measure, and his blood flowed in a kingly current. He was born a king. He came "to be ruler in Israel. "Ah!" says one, "then he came in vain, for little did he exercise his rule; 'he came unto his own, and his own received him not;' he came to Israel and he was not their ruler, but he was 'despised and rejected of men,' cast off by them all, and forsaken by Israel, unto whom he came." Ay, but "they are not all Israel who are of Israel," neither because they are the seed of Abraham shall they all be called. Ah, no! He is not ruler of Israel after the flesh, but he is the ruler of Israel after the spirit. Many such have obeyed him. Did not the apostles bow before him, and own him as their king? And now, doth not Israel salute him as their ruler? Do not all the seed of Abraham after the spirit, even all the faithful, for he is "the father of the faithful," acknowledge that unto Christ belong the shields of the mighty, for he is the king of the whole earth? Doth he not rule over Israel?

Ay, verily he doth; and those who are not ruled over by Christ are not of Israel. He came to be a ruler over Israel. My brother, hast thou submitted to the sway of Jesus? Is he ruler in thine heart, or is he not? We may know Israel by this: Christ is come into their hearts, to be ruler over them. "Oh!" saith one, "I do as I please, I was never in bondage to any man." Ah! then thou hatest the rule of Christ. "Oh!" says another, "I submit myself to my minister, to my clergyman, or to my priest, and I think that what he tells me is enough, for he is my ruler." Dost thou? Ah, poor slave, thou knowest not thy dignity; for nobody is thy lawful ruler but the Lord Jesus Christ. "Ay," says another, "I have professed his religion, and I am his follower." But doth he rule in thine heart? Doth he command thy will? Doth he guide thy judgment? Dost thou ever seek counsel at his hand in thy difficulties? Art thou desirous to honor him, and to put crowns upon his heart? Is he thy ruler? If so, then thou art one of Israel; for it is written, "He shall come to be ruler in Israel." Blessed Lord Jesus, thou art ruler in thy people's hearts, and thou ever shalt be; we want no other ruler save thyself, and we will submit to none other. We are free, because we are the servants of Christ; we are at liberty, because he is our ruler, and we know no bondage and no slavery, because Jesus Christ alone is monarch of our hearts. He came "to be ruler in Israel;" and mark you, that mission of his is not quite fulfilled yet, and shall not be till the latter-day glories. In a little while you shall see Christ come again, to be ruler over his people Israel, and ruler over them not only as spiritual Israel, but even as natural Israel, for the Jews shall be restored to their land, and the tribes of Jacob shall yet sing in the halls of their temple; unto God there shall yet again be offered Hebrew songs of praise, and the heart of the unbelieving Jew shall be melted at the feet of the true Messiah. In a short time, he who at his birth was hailed king of the Jews by Easterns, and at his death was written king of the Jews by a Western, shall be called king of the Jews everywhere—yes, king of the Jews and Gentiles also—in that universal monarchy whose dominion shall be co-extensive with the habitable globe, and whose duration shall be coeval with time itself. He came to be a ruler in Israel, and a ruler most decidedly he shall be, when he shall reign among his people with his ancients gloriously.

IV. And now, the last thing is, did Jesus Christ ever come before? We answer, yes, for our text says, "Whose goings forth have been of old, from everlasting."

First, Christ has had his goings forth in his Godhead. "From everlasting." He has not been a secret and a silent person up to this moment. That new-born child there has worked wonders long ere now; that infant slumbering in its mother's arms is the infant of today, but it is the ancient of eternity; that child who is there hath not made its appearance on the stage of this world; his name is not yet written in the calendar of the circumcised; but still though you wist it not, "his goings forth have been of old, from everlasting."

1. Of old he went forth as our covenant head in election, "according as he hath chosen us in Him, before the foundation of the world."

> "Christ be my first elect, he said,
> Then chose our souls in Christ our Head."

2. He had goings forth for his people, as their representative before the throne, even before they were begotten in the world. It was from everlasting that his mighty fingers grasped the pen, the stylus of ages, and wrote his own name, the name of the eternal Son of God; it was from everlasting that he signed the compact with his Father, that he would pay blood for blood, wound for wound, suffering for suffering, agony for agony, and death for death, in the behalf of his people; it was from everlasting that he gave himself up, without a murmuring word, that from the crown of his head to the sole of his foot he might sweat blood, that he might be spit upon, pierced, mocked, rent asunder, suffer the pain of death, and the agonies of the cross. His goings forth as our surety were from everlasting. Pause, my soul, and wonder! Thou hadst goings forth in the person of Jesus from everlasting. Not only when thou wast born into the world did Christ love thee, but his delights were with the sons of men before there were any sons of men. Often did he think of them; from everlasting to everlasting he had set his affection upon them. What! believer, has he been so long about thy salvation, and will he not accomplish it? Has he from everlasting been going forth to save me, and will he lose me now? What! has he had me in his hand, as his precious jewel, and will he now let me slip between his precious fingers? Did he choose me before the mountains were brought forth, or the channels of the deep scooped out, and will he lose me now? Impossible!

> "My name from the palms of his hands
>   Eternity cannot erase;
>   Impress'd on his heart it remains,
>   In marks of indelible grace."

I am sure he would not love me so long, and then leave off loving me. If he intended to be tired of me, he would have been tired of me long before now. If he had not loved me with a love as deep as hell and as unutterable as the grave, it he had not given his whole heart to me, I am sure he would have turned from me long ago. He knew what I would be, and he has had long time enough to consider of it; but I am his choice, and there is an end of it; and unworthy as I am, it is not mine to grumble, if he is but contented with me. But he is contented with me—he must be contented with me—for he has known me long enough to know my faults. He knew me before I knew myself; yea, he knew me before I was myself. Long before my members were fashioned they were written in his book, "when as yet there were none of them," his eyes of affection were set on them. He knew how badly I would act towards him, and yet he has continued to love me;

> "His love in times past forbids me to think.
>   He'll leave me at last in trouble to sink."

No, since "his goings forth were of old from everlasting," they will be "to everlasting."

   Secondly, we believe that Christ has come forth of old, even to men, so that men have beheld him. I will not stop to tell you that it was Jesus who walked in the garden of Eden in the cool of the day, for his delights were with the sons of men; nor will I detain you by pointing out all the various ways in which Christ came forth to his people in the form of the angel of the covenant, the Paschal Lamb, the and ten thousand types with which the sacred history is so replete; but I will rather point you to four occasions when Jesus Christ our Lord has appeared on earth as a man, before his great incarnation for our salvation. And, first, I beg to refer you to the 18th chapter of Genesis, where Jesus Christ appeared to Abraham, of whom we read, "The Lord appeared unto him in the plains of Mamre and he sat in the tent door in the heat of the day; and he lift up his eyes and looked, and lo, three men stood by him; and when he saw them, he ran to meet them from the tent door, and bowed himself toward the ground." But whom did he bow to? He said "My Lord," only to one of them. There was one man between the other two, the most conspicuous for his glory, for he was the God-man Christ; the other two were created angels, who for a time had assumed the appearance of men. But this was the man Christ Jesus.

> "And he said, My Lord, if now I have found favour in thy sight, pass not away, I pray thee, from thy servant. Let a little water, I pray you, be fetched, and wash your feet, and rest yourselves under the tree."

You will notice that this majestic man, this glorious person, stayed behind to talk with Abraham. In the 22nd verse it is said, — "And the men turned their faces from thence and went towards Sodom;" that is, two of them, as you will see in the next chapter—"but Abraham stood yet before the Lord." You will notice that this man, the Lord, held sweet fellowship with Abraham, and allowed Abraham to plead for the city he was about to destroy. He was in the positive form of man; so that when he walked the streets of Judea it was not the first time that he was a man; he was so before, in "the plain of Mamre, in the heat of the day." There is another instance—his appearing to Jacob, which you have recorded in the 32nd chapter of Genesis and the 24th verse. All his family were gone,

> "And Jacob was left alone, and there wrestled a man with him until the breaking of the day. And when he saw that he prevailed not against him, he touched the hollow of his thigh; and the hollow of Jacob's thigh was out of joint, as he wrestled with him. And he said, Let me go, for the day brea- keth. And he said, I will not let thee go, unless thou bless me. And he said unto him, What is thy name? And be said, Jacob. And he said, Thy name shall be called no more Jacob, but Israel; for as a prince hast thou power with God."

This was a man, and yet God. "For as a prince hast thou power with God and with men, and hast prevailed." And Jacob knew that this man was God, for he says in the 30th verse, "for I have seen God face to face and my life is preserved." Another instance you will find in the book of Joshua when Joshua had crossed the narrow stream of Jordan, and had entered the promised land, and was about to drive out the Canaanites. Lo, this mighty man-God ap- peared to Joshua. In the 5th chapter, at the 13th verse, we read, "And it came to pass, when Joshua was by Jericho, that he lifted up his eyes and looked, and, behold, there stood a man over against him with his sword drawn in his hand, and Joshua went unto him, and (like a brave warrior, as he was,) said unto him, Art thou for us, or for our adversaries? And he said, Nay; but as captain of the host of the Lord am I now come." And Joshua saw at once that there was divinity in him; for Joshua fell on his face to the earth, and did worship, and said to him, "What saith my Lord unto his servant?" Now, if this had been a created angel he would have reproved Joshua, and said, "I am one of your fellow servants." But no; "the captain of the Lord's host said unto Joshua, Loose thy shoe from thy foot; for the place whereon thou standest is holy. And Joshua did so." Another remarkable instance is that recorded in the third chapter of the book of Daniel, where we read the account of Shadrach, Meshach, and Abednego being cast into the fiery furnace, which was so fierce that it destroyed the men who threw them in. Suddenly the king said to his counsellors, "Did not we cast three men bound into the midst of the fire? They answered and said unto the king, True, king. He answered and said, Lo, I see four men loose, walking in the midst of the fire, and they have no hurt; and the form of the fourth is like the Son of God." How should Nebuchadnezzar know that? Only that there was something so noble and majestic in the way in which that wondrous Man bore himself, and some awful influence about him, who so marvellously broke the consuming teeth of that biting an I devouring flame, so that it could not so much as singe the children of God. Nebuchadnezzar recognized his humanity. He did not say,"I see three men and an angel," but he said, "I see four positive men, and the form of the fourth is like the Son of God." You see, then, what is meant by his goings forth being "from everlasting."

Observe for a moment here, that each of these four great occurrences happened to the saints when they were engaged in very eminent duty, or when they were about to be engaged in it. Jesus Christ does not appear to his saints every day. He did not come to see Jacob till he was in affliction; he did not visit Joshua before he was about to be engaged in a righteous war. It is only in extraordinary seasons that Christ thus manifests himself to his people. When Abraham interceded for Sodom, Jesus was with him, for one of the highest and noblest employments of a Christian is that of intercession, and it is when he is so engaged that he will be likely to obtain a sight of Christ. Jacob was engaged in wrestling, and that is a part of a Christian's duty to which some of you never did attain;

consequently, you do not have many visits from Jesus. It was when Joshua was exercising bravery that the Lord met him. So with Shadrach, Meshach, and Abednego; they were in the high places of persecution, on account of their adherence to duty, when he came to them, and said, "I will be with you, passing through the fire." There are certain peculiar places we must enter, to meet with the Lord. We must be in great trouble, like Jacob; we must be in great labour, like Joshua; we must have great intercessory faith, like Abraham; we must be firm in the performance of duty, like Shadrach, Meshach, and Abednego, or else we shall not know him, whose goings forth have been of old, "from everlasting;" or, if we know him, we shall not be able to "comprehend with all the saints what is the height, and depth, and length, and breadth of the love of Christ, which passeth knowledge."

Sweet Lord Jesus! Thou whose goings forth were of old, even from everlasting, thou hast not left thy goings forth yet. Oh, that thou wouldst go forth this day, to cheer the faint, to help the weary, to bind up our wounds, to comfort our distresses! Go forth, we beseech thee, to conquer sinners, to subdue hard hearts, to break the iron gates of sinners' lusts, and cut the iron bars of their sins in pieces! O Jesus, go forth; and when thou goest forth, come thou to me! Am I a hardened sinner? Come thou to me; I want thee:

"Oh! let thy grace my heart subdue;
I would be led in triumph too;
A willing captive to my Lord,
To sing the honours of thy word."

Poor sinner! Christ has not left going forth yet. And when he goes forth, recollect, he goes to Bethlehem. Have you a Bethlehem in your heart? Are you little? He will go forth to you yet. Go home and seek him by earnest prayer. If you have been made to weep on account of sin, and think yourself too little to be noticed, go home, little one! Jesus comes to little ones; his goings forth were of old, and he is going forth now. He will come to your poor old house; he will come to your poor wretched heart; he will come, though you are in poverty, and clothed in rags, though you are destitute, tormented, and afflicted; he will come, for his goings forth have been of old from everlasting. Trust him, trust him, trust him; and he will go forth to abide in your heart for ever.

VII. God Incarnate, The End of Fear

"And the angel said unto them, Fear not."
Luke 2:10.

No sooner did the angel of the Lord appear to the shepherds, and the glory of the Lord shone round about them, than they were sorely afraid. It had come to this, that man was afraid of his God, and when God sent down His loving messengers with tidings of great joy, men were filled with as much fright as though the angel of Death had appeared with uplifted sword. The silence of night and its dreary gloom caused no fear in the shepherds' hearts, but the joyful herald of the skies, robed in mildest glories of divine grace, made them afraid.

We must not condemn the shepherds on this account as though they were peculiarly timid or ignorant, for they were only acting as every other person in that age would have done under the same circumstances. Not because they were simple shepherds amazed with fear, but it is probable that if they had been well-instructed prophets they would have displayed the same feeling. There are many instances recorded in Scripture in which the foremost men of their time trembled and felt a horror of great darkness when special manifestations of God were vouchsafed to them. In fact, a slavish fear of God was so common that a tradition had grown out of it, which was all but universally received as nothing less than the Truth of God.

It was generally believed that every supernatural manifestation was to be regarded as a token of speedy death. "We shall surely die because we have seen God" was not only Manoah's conclusion, but that of most men of his period. Few, indeed, were those happy minds who, like Manoah's wife, could reason in a more cheerful style, "If the Lord had meant to destroy us He would not have showed us such things as these." It became the settled conviction of all men, whether wise or simple, whether good or bad, that a manifestation of God was not so much to be rejoiced in as to be dreaded. Even Jacob said, "How dreadful is this place! It is none other but the house of God."

Doubtless the spirit which originated this tradition was much fostered by the legal dispensation which is better fitted for trembling servants than for rejoicing sons. It was of the bond woman and it gendered into bondage. The solemn night in which its greatest institution was ordained was a night of trembling. Death was there in the slaughter of the lamb. Blood was there sprinkled on a conspicuous part of the house. Fire was there to roast the lamb—all the emblems of judgment were there to strike the mind with awe. It was at the dread hour of midnight when the solemn family conclave was assembled. The door being shut, the guests, themselves, standing in an uneasy attitude, and awe-stricken, for their hearts could hear the wings of the destroying angel as he passed by the house.

Afterwards, when Israel came into the wilderness, and the law was proclaimed, do we not read that the people stood afar off and that bounds were set about the mount? And if so much as a beast touched the mountain it was to be stoned or thrust through with a dart! It was a day of fear and trembling when God spoke to them out of the fire. Not with the melting notes of harp, psaltery, or dulcimer did God's law come to His people's ears! No soft wings of angels brought the message, and no sunny smiles of heaven sweetened it to the mind! No, with sound of trumpet and thunder, out of the midst of blazing lightning—with Sinai altogether on a smoke—the law was given.

The law's voice was, "Come not near here!" The spirit of Sinai is fear and trembling. The legal ceremonies were such as rather to inspire fear than to beget trust. The worshipper at the temple saw bloodshed from the first of the year to the end of the year. The morning was ushered in with the blood-shedding of the lamb, and the evening shades could not gather without blood again being spilt upon the altar! God was in the midst of the camp, but the pillar of cloud and fire was His unapproachable pavilion.

The emblem of His glory was concealed behind the curtain of blue and scarlet and fine twined linen—behind which only one foot might pass—and that but once in the year. Men spoke of the God of Israel with bated breath and with voices hushed and solemn. They had not learned to say, "Our Father which art in heaven." They had not received the spirit of adoption, and were not able to say

"Abba, Father." They smarted under the spirit of bondage which made them sorely afraid when by any peculiar manifestation the Lord displayed His presence among
them. At the bottom of all this slavish dread lay sin.

We never find Adam afraid of God, nor of any manifestation of deity while he was an obedient creature in paradise. But no sooner had he touched the fatal fruit than he
found that he was naked and hid himself! When he heard
the voice of the Lord God walking in the garden in the
cool of the day, Adam was afraid and hid himself from
the presence of the Lord God among the trees of the garden. Sin makes miserable cowards of us all! See the man
who once could hold delightful converse with his maker
now dreading to hear his maker's voice and skulking in
the grove like a felon who knows his guilt, and is afraid to
meet the officers of justice!

Beloved, in order to remove this dread nightmare of
slavish fear from the breast of humanity, where its horrible influence represses all the noblest aspirations of the
soul, our Lord Jesus Christ came in the flesh! This is one
of the works of the devil which He was manifested to destroy. Angels came to proclaim the good news of the advent of the Incarnate God, and the very first note of their
song was a foretaste of the sweet result of His coming to
all those who shall receive Him. The angel said, "Fear
not," as though the times of fear were over, and the days
of hope and joy had arrived! "Fear not." These words were
not meant for those trembling shepherds, only, but were
intended for you and for me, yes, for all nations to whom
the glad tidings shall come. "Fear not." Let God no longer
be the object of your slavish dread! Stand not at a distance
from Him any more. The Word is made flesh. God has descended to tabernacle among men, that there may be no
hedge of fire, no yawning gulf between God and man.

Into this subject I wish to go this morning as God may
help me. I am sensible of the value of the theme, and am
very conscious that I cannot do it justice. I would earnestly
ask God the Holy Spirit to make you drink of the golden
cup of the incarnation of Christ such draughts as I have en-
joyed in my quiet meditations. I can scarcely desire more
delight for my dearest friends.

There is no antidote for fear more excellent than the
subject of that midnight song, the first and best of Christmas chorales, which from its first word to its last note
chimes out the sweet message, which begins with, "Fear

not." —

> "It is my sweetest comfort, Lord,
> And will forever be,
> To muse upon the gracious truth
> Of your humanity.
>
> Oh joy! There sits in our flesh,
> Upon a throne of light,
> One of a human mother born,
> In perfect Godhead bright!
>
> Though earth's foundations should be moved,
> Down to their lowest deep.
> Though all the trembling universe
> Into destruction sweep.
>
> Forever God, forever man,
> My Jesus shall endure.
> And fixed on Him,
> My hope remains eternally secure."

Dear friends, I shall first detain your attention with a few remarks upon the fear of which I have already spoken. Then, secondly, we shall invite your earnest attention to the remedy which the angels came to proclaim. And then, thirdly, as we may have time, we shall endeavor to make an application of this remedy to various cases.

I. Turning to the fear of the text, it may be well to discriminate. There is a kind of fear towards God from which we must not wish to be free. There is that lawful, necessary, admirable, excellent fear which is always due from the creature to the creator, from the subject to the king, yes, and from the child toward the parent. That holy, filial fear of God, which makes us dread sin and constrains us to be obedient to His command is to be cultivated. "We had fathers of our flesh, and we gave them reverence, shall we not be in subjection to the Father of spirits and live?" This is the "fear of the Lord which is the beginning of wisdom." To have a holy awe of our most holy, just, righteous, and tender parent is a privilege, not a bondage! Godly fear is not the "fear which has torment." Perfect love does not cast out, but dwells in joyful harmony. The angels perfectly love God, and yet with holy fear they veil their faces with their wings as they approach Him. And when we shall in glory behold the face of God, and shall be filled with all His fullness, we shall not cease humbly and reverently to adore the infinite majesty. Holy fear is a work of the Holy Spirit, and woe unto the man who does not possess it! Let him boast as he may, his "feeding himself without fear" is a mark of his hypocrisy!

The fear which is to be avoided, is slavish fear—the fear which perfect love casts out, as Sarah cast out the bondwoman and her son. That trembling which keeps us at a distance from God, which makes us think of Him as a Spirit with whom we can have no communion—as a being who has no care for us except to punish us—and for whom, consequently, we have no care except to escape if possible from His terrible presence. This fear sometimes arises in men's hearts from their thoughts dwelling exclusively upon the divine greatness. Is it possible to peer long into the vast abyss of infinity and not to fear? Can the mind yield itself up to the thought of the eternal, self-existent, infinite one without being filled, first with awe and then with dread? What am I? An aphid creeping upon a rosebud is a more considerable creature in relation to the universe of beings than I can be in comparison with God! What am I? A grain of dust that does not turn the scale of the most delicate balance is a greater thing to man than a man is to Jehovah! At best we are less than nothing and vanity! But there is more to abase us than this. We have had the impertinence to be disobedient to the will of this great one! And now the goodness and greatness of His nature are as a current against which sinful humanity struggles in vain, for the irresistible torrent must run its course and overwhelm every opponent. What does the great God seem to us, out of Christ, but a stupendous rock threatening to crush us, or a fathomless sea, hastening to swallow us up?

The contemplation of the divine greatness may of itself fill man with horror and cast him into unutterable misery! Dwell long upon such themes, and like Job, you will tremble before Jehovah, who shakes the earth out of her place, and makes the pillars tremble. Each one of the sterner attributes of God will cause the same fear. Think of His power by which He rolls the stars along, and lay your hand upon your mouth. Think of His wisdom by which He numbers the clouds, and settles the ordinances of Heaven. Meditate upon any one of these attributes, but especially upon His justice, and upon that devouring fire which burns unceasingly against sin—and it is no wonder if the soul becomes full of fear. Meanwhile let a sense of sin with its great whip of wire flagellate the conscience, and man will dread the bare idea of God. For this is the burden of the voice of conscience to guilty man—

> "If thou wert an obedient creature, this God were still terrible to thee, for the heavens are not pure in his sight, and he charged his angels with folly. What art thou that thou shouldst be just with God, or have any claims upon him; for thou hast offended, thou hast lifted the hand of thy rebellion against the infinite majesty of omnipotence — what can become of thee? what can be thy portion but to be set up for ever as a monument of his righteous wrath?"

Now such a fear as that being very easily created in the thoughtful mind, and being, indeed, as it seems to me, the natural heritage of man as the result of sin is most doleful and injurious. For wherever there is a slavish dread of the divine being it alienates man most thoroughly from his God. We are by our evil nature enemies to God, and the imagination that God is cruel, harsh, and terrible adds fuel to the fire of our enmity. Those whom we slavishly dread we cannot love. You could not make your child show forth love to you if its little heart was full of fear—if it dreaded to hear your footsteps and was alarmed at the sound of your voice it could not love you. You might obey some huge monster because you were afraid of him, but to love him would be impossible.

It is one of the masterpieces of Satan to deceive man by presenting to his mind a hateful picture of God. He knows that men cannot love that which terrifies them and therefore he paints the God of grace as a hard, unforgiving being who will not receive the penitent and have pity upon the sorrowful. God is love! Surely if men had but grace enough to see the beauty of that portrait of God— that miniature sketched with a single line, "God is love!" they would willingly serve such a God. When the Holy Spirit enables the mind to perceive the character of God, the heart cannot refuse to love Him. Base, fallen, depraved as men are, when they are illuminated from on high so as to judge rightly of God, their hearts melt under the genial beams of divine love and they love God because He has first loved them. But there is the masterpiece of Satan, that he will not let the understanding perceive the excellence of God's character and then the heart cannot love that which the understanding does not perceive to be loveable. In addition to alienating the heart from God, this fear creates a prejudice against God's gospel of grace. There are persons in this place this morning who believe that if they were religious they would be miserable. It is the settled conviction of half of London that to trust in Jesus and to be obedient to God, which is the essence of all true religion, would be wretchedness itself. "Oh," says the worldly man, "I should have to give up my pleasure if I were to become a Christian." Now this is one of the most wicked slanders that was ever invented and yet it has current belief everywhere. It is the popular theology that to be an enemy to God is happiness, but to be the friend of God is misery. What an opinion men must have of God, when they believe that to love Him is to be wretched! Oh, could they comprehend, could they but know how good God is—instead of imagining that His service would be slavery, they would understand that to be His friend is to occupy the highest and happiest position which created beings can occupy.

This fear in some men puts them out of all hope of ever being saved. Thinking God to be an ungenerous being, they keep at a distance from Him. If there are some sweet attractions, now and then in a sermon, some gentle meltings of conscience, the good desire never matures into the practical resolve. They do not say, "I will arise and go unto my Father," because they do not know Him as a Father—they only know Him as a consuming fire. A man does not say, "I will arise and go unto a consuming fire." No, but like Jonah, he would gladly pay his fare, regardless of the expense, and go to Tarshish to flee from the presence of the Lord! This it is that makes calamity of being a man at all, to most men—that they cannot get away from God, since they imagine that if they could but escape from His presence they would then wander into bliss. But being doomed to be where God is, they then conceive that for them wretchedness and misery alone remain. The soft warnings of mercy and the thundering of justice are, alike, powerless upon men so long as their hearts are seared and rendered callous by an unholy dread of God.

This wicked dread of God frequently drives men to extremities of sin. The man says, "There is no hope for me. I have made one fatal mistake in being God's enemy and I am irretrievably ruined. There is no hope that I shall ever be restored to happiness or peace. Then what will I do? I will cast the reins upon the neck of my passions. I will defy fate and take my chance. I will get such happiness as may be found in sin. If I cannot be reconciled to heaven I will be a good servant of hell." And therefore men have been known to hasten from one crime to another with a malicious inventiveness of rebellion against God. They act as if they could never be satisfied nor contented till they had heaped up more and more rebellions against the majesty of God whom in their hearts they dread with a burning satanic dread mingled with hate. If they could but comprehend that He is still willing to receive the rebellious, that His heart yearns towards sinners. If they could but once believe that He is love and wills not the death of a sinner but had rather that he should turn unto Him and live, surely the course of their lives must be changed. But the god of this world blinds them and maligns the Lord until they count it folly to submit to Him.

Dear friends, this evil which works a thousand ills operates in ways of evil quite innumerable. It dishonors God. Oh, it is infamous! It is villainous to make out our God, who is light and in whom is no darkness at all, to be an object of horrible fear. It is infernal! I may say no less. It is devilish to the highest degree to paint Him as a demon, who is Jehovah, the God of love. Oh, the impertinence of the prince of darkness, and the madness of man to consent to him, that God should be depicted as being unwilling to forgive, unkind, untender, hard, cruel—whereas He is love—supremely and above all things, love. He is just, but all the more truly loving because He is just. He is true, and therefore sure to punish sin, yet even punishing sin because it were not good to let sin go unpunished. This is base ingratitude on the part of a much-receiving creature that he should malign his benefactor. The evil which is thus done to God recoils upon man—for this fear has torment. No more tormenting misery in the world than to think of God as being our implacable foe. You Christians who have lost, for a while, the spirit of adoption—you who have wandered a distance from God and nothing can be more tormenting to you than the fear that the Lord has cast you away and will not again receive you. You backsliders, nothing can hold you back from your heavenly Father like a dread of Him. If you can but really know that He is not to be dreaded with slavish fear, you will come to Him as your child does to you, and you will say, "My Father, I have offended—pity me! My Father, I am vexed and grieved for my sin—forgive me, receive me again to Your arms, and help me, by Your mighty grace, that from now

on I may walk in Your commandments and be obedient
to Your will." My dear friends, you who know anything
about spiritual life—don't you feel that when you have
sweet thoughts of God breathed into you from above and
have His special love to you shed abroad in your hearts—
don't you feel that it is then that you are most holy? Have
you not perceived that the only way in which you can
grow in that which is morally and spiritually lovely, is by
having your gracious God high in your esteem, and feeling His precious love firing your hearts? That they may be
like little children is the very thing which God desires for
His elect ones! It is this which His Spirit works in His chosen! It is to this that we must come if we are to be meet to
be partakers of the inheritance of the saints in light. Slavish fear is so opposed to the child-like spirit that it is as the
poison of asps to it. Dread and fear bring out everything in
us that is of the man rather than of the child, for it stirs us
up to resist the object of our fear. An assured confidence
in the goodness of God casts out fear and brings forth
everything that is child-like in us. Have you ever seen a
child trust some big, rough man, and melt him down by
its trustfulness? It trusted where there was no ground for
trust, apparently, and made ground for itself. That same
child, simply and implicitly trusting in a good and gener-
ous father is a noble picture. And if I, a poor, weak, feeble
child, conscious that I am such—knowing that I am all folly and weakness—can just believe in my good, great God,
through Jesus Christ, and come and trust myself with Him
and leave Him to do as He likes with me, believing that He
will not be unkind, and cannot be unwise—if I can wholly
repose in His love and be obedient to His will—why then
I shall have reached the highest point that the creature can
reach! The Holy Spirit will then have worked His finished
work in me and I shall be fit for heaven. Beloved, it is because fear opposes this, and prevents this, that I would say
with the angel, "Fear not."

II. I fear I weary you while I speak upon this somewhat
dolorous theme, and therefore with as much brevity as the
abundance of the matter may permit, let us notice in the
second place, the cure for this fear, which the angel came
to proclaim. It lies in this—"Unto you is born this day in
the city of David, a savior, which is Christ the Lord."—

"Till God in human flesh I see,
My thoughts no comfort find.
The holy, just and sacred Three,

Are terrors to my mind.
But if Immanuel's face appears,
My hope, my joy begins!
His name forbids my slavish fear,
His grace removes my sins."

That is the remedy—God with us—God made flesh. Let us
try and show this from the angel's song. According to the
text they were not to fear, first of all, because the angel had
come to bring them good news. How does it run? It says,
"I bring you good tidings of great joy." But what was this
Gospel? Further on we are told that the Gospel was the fact
that Christ was born! So, then, it is good news to men that
Christ is born, that God has come down and taken manhood into union with Himself. Verily this is glad tidings!
He who made the heavens slumbers in a manger. What
then? Why, then God is not of necessity an enemy to man
because here is God actually taking manhood into alliance
with deity! There cannot be permanent, inveterate, rooted
enmity between the two natures, or otherwise the divine
nature could not have taken the human into hypostatical
union with itself. Is there not comfort in that? You are a
poor, erring, feeble man, and that which makes you afraid
of the Lord is this fear that there is an enmity between God
and man—but there need not be such enmity—for your
maker has actually taken manhood into union with Himself. Do you not see another thought? The eternal seems to
be so far away from us. He is infinite and we are such little
creatures. There appears to be a great gulf fixed between
man and God, even on the ground of creatureship. But
observe, He who is God has also become man. We never
heard that God took the nature of angels into union with
Himself—we may therefore say that between Godhead
and angelhood there must be an infinite distance still—but
here the Lord has actually taken manhood into union with
Himself. There is, therefore, no longer a great gulf fixed.
On the contrary, here is a marvelous union. Godhead has
entered into marriage bonds with manhood.

O my soul, you do not stand, now, like a poor lone
orphan wailing across the deep sea after your Father who
has gone far away and cannot hear you. You do not now
sob and sigh like an infant left naked and helpless, its maker having gone too far away to regard its needs or listen to
its cries! No, your maker has become like yourself! Is that
too strong a word to use? He without whom was not anything made that was made is that same Word who lived

and walked among us and was made flesh—made flesh
in such a way that He was tempted in all points like as
we are—yet without sin. O manhood, was there ever such
news as this for you. Poor manhood, you weak worm of
the dust—far lower than the angels—lift up your head and
be not afraid. Poor manhood, born in weakness, living in
toil, covered with sweat, and dying at last to be eaten by
the worms—be not abashed even in the presence of ser-
aphs—for next to God is man, and not even an archangel
can come in between. No, not next to God, there is scarcely
that to be said, for Jesus who is God is man also. Jesus
Christ, eternally God, was born and lived and died as we
also do. That is the first word of comfort to expel our fear.

The second point that takes away fear is that this man
who was also God was actually born. Observe the angel's
word, "Unto you is born." Our Lord Jesus Christ is in some
senses more man than Adam. Adam was not born—Adam
never had to struggle through the risks and weaknesses
of infancy. He knew not the littlenesses of childhood—he
was full grown at once. Father Adam could not sympa-
thize with me as a babe and a child. But how man-like is
Jesus! He is cradled with us in the manger. He does not
begin with us in mid-life, as Adam, but He accompanies
us in the pains and feebleness and infirmities of infancy!
And He continues with us even to the grave.

Beloved, this is such sweet comfort. He that is God
this day was once an infant! So that if my cares are little
and even trivial and comparatively infantile, I may go to
Him, for He was once a child. Though the great ones of
the earth may sneer at the child of poverty, and say, "You
are too mean, and your trouble is too slight for pity," I remember with humble joy that the king of heaven did hang
upon a woman's breast, and was wrapped in swaddling
bands—and therefore I tell Him all my griefs. How wonderful that He should have been an infant, and yet should
be God over all, blessed forever. I am no longer afraid
of God. This blessed link between me and God, the holy
Child Jesus, has taken all fear away.

Observe, the angel told them somewhat of His office,
as well as of His birth. "Unto you is born this day a savior." The very object for which He was born and came into
this world was that He might deliver us from sin. What,
then, was it that made us afraid? Were we not afraid of
God because we felt that we were lost through sin? Well
then, here is joy upon joy. Here is not only the Lord come

among us as a man, but made man in order to save man from that which separated him from God. I feel as if I could burst out into a weeping for some here who have been spending their living riotously and gone far away from God their Father by their evil ways. I know they are afraid to come back. They think that the Lord will not receive them, that there is no mercy for such sinners as they have been. Oh, but think of it—Jesus Christ has come to seek and to save that which was lost. He was born to save. If He does not save He was born in vain, for the object of His birth was salvation! If He shall not be a savior, then the mission of God to earth has missed its end, for its design was that lost sinners might be saved.

Lost one, oh, lost one!—if there were news that an angel had come to save you there might be some cheer in it. But there are better tidings still. God has come! The infinite, the almighty, has stooped from the highest heaven that He may pick you up, a poor undone and worthless worm. Is there not comfort here? Does not the incarnate savior take away the horrible dread which hangs over men like a black pall? Note that the angel did not forget to describe the person of this Savior—"A savior which is Christ." There is His manhood! As man He was anointed! "The Lord." There is His Godhead. Yes, this is the solid truth of God upon which we plant our feet. Jesus of Nazareth is God! He who was conceived in the womb of the virgin and born in Bethlehem's manger is now, and always was God over all, blessed forever! There is no Gospel if He is not God. It is no news to me to tell me that a great prophet is born. There have been great prophets before. But the world has never been redeemed from evil by mere testimony to the truth, and never will be. Tell me that God is born, that God, Himself, has espoused our nature, and taken it into union with Himself. Then the bells of my heart ring merry peals, for now may I come to God since God has come to me.

You will observe, dear friends, that the substance of what the angel said lay in this, "Unto you." You will never get true comfort from the incarnate savior till you perceive your personal interest in him. Christ as Man was a representative man. There never were but two thoroughly representative men—the first is Adam—Adam obedient and the whole race stands. Adam disobedient and the whole race falls. "In Adam all die." Now, the man Jesus is the second great representative man. He does not represent the whole human race—He represents as many as His Father gave Him—He represents a chosen company.

Now, whatever Christ did, if you belong to those who are in Him, He did for you. So that Christ circumcised or Christ crucified, Christ dead or Christ living, Christ buried or Christ risen, you are a partaker of all that He did and all that He is, for you are reckoned as one with Him. See then, the joy and comfort of the incarnation of Christ. Does Jesus, as man, take manhood up to heaven? He has taken me up there. Father Adam fell, and I fell, for I was in him. The Lord Jesus Christ rises, and I rise if I am in Him. See, beloved, when Jesus Christ was nailed to the cross all His elect were nailed there, and they suffered and died in Him. When He was put into the grave the whole of His people lay slumbering there in Him, for they were in the loins of Jesus as Levi was in the loins of Abraham. And when He rose they rose and received the foretaste of their own future resurrection. Because He lives they shall live also. And now that He has gone up on high to claim the throne, He has claimed the throne for every soul that is in Him. Oh, this is joy, indeed. Then how can I be afraid of God, for this day, by faith, I, a poor undeserving sinner, having put my trust in Jesus, am bold to say that I sit upon the throne of God? Think not that we have said too much, for in the person of Christ every believer is raised up together, and made to sit together in heavenly places in Christ Jesus. Because as Jesus is there representatively, we are each one of us there in Him.

I wish that I had power to bring out this precious doctrine of the incarnation as I desire, but the more one muses upon it, the more happy one becomes. Let us view it as an all-important truth of God that Jesus, the Son of God, has really come in the flesh. It is so important a truth that we have three witnesses appointed to keep it before us upon earth. We have been insisting many times in this place upon the spirituality of Christian worship. We have shown that the outward in religion, by itself, avails nothing. It is the inward spirit that is the great thing.

I must confess that I have sometimes said in myself, I hope not rebelliously, "What is this baptism for, and what is this communion of the Lord's Supper for?" These two outward ordinances, whatever may be their excellent uses, have been the two things around which more errors have clustered than around anything else! And I have heard it said, by friends inclined to follow more fully the teachings of the Quakers, "Why not put aside the outward and visible altogether? Let it be the Spirit baptism, and not the water. Let there be no bread and wine, but let there be fellowship with Christ without the outward sign." I must confess, though I dare not go with it because I hope to be held fast by the plain testimony of Scripture, yet my heart has somewhat gone with the temptation and I have half said, "Men always will pervert these two ordinances. Would it not be as well to have done with them?" While I have been exercised upon the point, conscious that the ordinances must be right, and must be held, I have rested upon that text, "There are three that bear witness in earth, the Spirit, the water, and the blood." And what do they bear witness to? They bear witness to the mission of Jesus as the Christ, in other words, to the real incarnation of God. They bear witness to the materialism of Christ. Have you ever noticed that when people have given up the two outward ordinances, they have usually betrayed a tendency to give up the literal fact that "God was made flesh"? The literal fact that Christ was really a Man has generally been doubted or thrown into the background when the two outward ordinances have been given up. I believe that these two symbolical ordinances, which are a link between the spiritual and the material, are set up on purpose to show that Christ Jesus, though most gloriously a Spirit, was also a Man clothed in a body of real flesh and blood like our own, so that He could be touched and handled even as He said, "Handle Me and see. A spirit has not flesh and bones as you see I have."

When I think of the Holy Spirit who bears witness that Christ was really a man, I thank Him for that witness. Then I turn to the water, and when I read that Christ was publicly baptized in the Jordan, I perceive that He could not have been a phantom. He could not have been a mere spectral appearance, for He was immersed in water. He must have been a solid substantial man. The preservation of the ordinance of baptism is a witness to the reality of the incarnate God. Then comes the blood. He could not have shed blood on Calvary if He had been a specter. There could have been no blood streaming down from His side when the spear pierced Him if He had been only a ghostly apparition. He must have been solid flesh and blood like ourselves—and as often as we come to His table, and we take the cup and hear it said—"This cup is the new covenant in my blood"—there is a third witness on earth to the

fact that Jesus did appear in very flesh and blood among
men.

So the Spirit, the water, and the blood are the three
standing testimonies in the church of God that Christ was
God, and that He was also really, solidly, and substan-
tially man. I shall delight in the ordinances all the more
because of this. Those two ordinances serve to make us
remember that Christ was really flesh and blood, and that
religion has something to do with this flesh and blood of
ours. This very body is to rise again from the tomb. Jesus
came to deliver this poor flesh from corruption. And so,
while we must ever keep the spiritual uppermost, we are
prevented from casting away the material body as though
that were of the devil. Christ purified as well the realm of
matter as the realm of spirit. And in both He reigns trium-
phant. There is much comfort here.

III. Lastly, we can only occupy a few seconds in ap-
plying the cure to various cases. Child of God, you say,
"I dare not come to God today, I feel so weak." Fear not,
for He that is born in Bethlehem said, "A bruised reed I
will not break, and the smoking flax I will not quench." "I
shall never get to heaven," says another, "I shall never see
God's face with acceptance. I am so tempted." "Fear not,"
for you have not an high priest which cannot be touched
with a feeling of your infirmities, for He was tempted in all
points like as you are." "But I am so lonely in the world,"
says another, "no man cares for me." There is one man, at
any rate, who does so care—a true man like yourself. He
is your brother, still, and does not forget the lonely spirit. But I hear a sinner say, "I am afraid to go to God this
morning and confess that I am a sinner." Well, do not go
to God but go to Christ. Surely you would not be afraid
of Him. Think of God in Christ, not out of Christ. If you
could but know Jesus you would go to Him at once. You
would not be afraid to tell Him your sins, for you would
know that He would say, "Go and sin no more." "I cannot pray," says one, "I am afraid to pray." What? Afraid
to pray when it is a man who listens to you. You might
dread the face of God, but when you see God in human
flesh, why be alarmed? Go, poor Sinner, go to Jesus. "I
feel," says one, "unfit to come." You may be unfit to come
to God, but you cannot be unfit to come to Jesus. There
is a fitness necessary to stand in the holy hill of the Lord,
but there is no fitness needed in coming to the Lord Jesus.
Come as you are—guilty, and lost, and ruined. Come just

as you are and He will receive you. "Oh," says another, "I cannot trust." I can understand your not being able to trust the great invisible God, but cannot you trust that dying, bleeding Son of Man who is also the Son of God? "But I cannot hope," says another, "that He would even look on me." And yet He used to look on such as you are. He received publicans and sinners and ate with them. And even harlots were not driven from His presence. Oh, since God has thus taken man into union with Himself be not afraid. If I speak to one who by reason of sin has wandered so far away from God that he is even afraid to think of God's name, yet inasmuch as Jesus Christ is called "the sinner's friend," I pray you think of Him, poor soul, as your friend.

And, oh, may the Spirit of God open your blind eyes to see that there is no cause for your keeping away from God except your own mistaken thoughts of Him. May you believe that He is able and willing to save to the uttermost. May you understand His good and gracious character, His readiness to pass by transgression, iniquity, and sin. And may the sweet influences of divine grace quicken you to come to Him this very morning. God grant that Jesus Christ, the hope of glory, may be formed in you. And then you may well sing, "Glory to God in the highest; on earth peace, and goodwill toward men." Amen.

VIII. A Christmas Question

"For unto us a child is born, unto us a son is given."
Isaiah 9:6.

Upon other occasions I have explained the main part of this verse—"the government shall be upon his shoulders, his name shall be called Wonderful, Counsellor, the Mighty God." If God shall spare me, on some future occasion I hope to take the other titles, "The Everlasting Father, the Prince of Peace." But now this morning the portion which will engage our attention is this, "Unto us a child is born, unto us a Son is given." The sentence is a double one, but it has in it no tautology. The careful reader will soon discover a distinction; and it is not a distinction without a difference. "Unto us a child is born, unto us a Son is given." As Jesus Christ is a child in his human nature, he is born, begotten of the Holy Ghost, born of the virgin Mary. He is as truly-born, as certainly a child, as any other man that ever lived upon the face of the earth. He is thus in his humanity a child born. But as Jesus Christ is God's Son, he is not born; but given, begotten of his Father from before all worlds, begotten—not made, being of the same substance with the Father. The doctrine of the eternal affiliation of Christ is to be received as an undoubted truth of our holy religion. But as to any explanation of it, no man should venture thereon, for it remaineth among the deep things of God—one of those solemn mysteries indeed, into which the angels dare not look, nor do they desire to pry into it—a mystery which we must not attempt to fathom, for it is utterly beyond the grasp of any finite being. As well might a gnat seek to drink in the ocean, as a finite creature to comprehend the Eternal God. A God whom we could understand would be no God. If we could grasp him he could not be infinite: if we could understand him, then were he not divine. Jesus Christ then, I say, as a Son, is not born to us, but given. He is a boon bestowed on us, "For God so loved the world, that he sent his only begotten Son into the world." He was not born in this world as God's

104

Son, but he was sent, or was given, so that you clearly perceive that the distinction is a suggestive one, and conveys much good truth to us. "Unto us a child is born, unto us a Son is given."

This morning, however, the principal object of my discourse, and, indeed, the sole one, is to bring out the force of those two little words, "unto us." For you will perceive that here the full force of the passage lies. "For unto us a child is born, unto us a Son is given." The divisions of my discourse are very simple ones. First, is it so? Secondly, if it is so, what then? Thirdly, if it is not so, what then?

I. In the first place, is it so? Is it true that unto us a child is born, unto us a Son is given? It is a fact that a child is born. Upon that I use no argument. We receive it as a fact, more fully established than any other fact in history, that the Son of God became man, was born at Bethlehem, wrapped in swaddling clothes, and laid in a manger. It is a fact, too, that a Son is given. About that we have no question. The infidel may dispute, but we, professing to be believers in Scripture, receive it as an undeniable truth, that God has given his only begotten Son to be the savior of men. But the matter of question is this: Is this child born to us? Is he given to us? This is the matter of anxious enquiry. Have we a personal interest in the child that was born at Bethlehem? Do we know that he is our savior?—that he has brought glad tidings to us?—that to us he belongs and that we belong to him? I say this is matter of very grave and solemn investigation. It is a very observable fact, that the very best of men are sometimes troubled with questions with regard to their own interest in Christ, while men who never are troubled at all about the matter are very frequently presumptuous deceivers, who have no part in this matter. I have often observed that some of the people about whom I felt most sure, were the very persons who were the least sure of themselves. It reminds me of the history of a godly man named Simon Brown, a minister in the olden times in the city of London. He became so extremely sad in heart, so depressed in spirit, that at last he conceived the idea that his soul was annihilated. It was all in vain to talk to the good man, you could not persuade him that he had a soul; but all the time he was preaching, and praying, and working, more like a man that had two souls than none. When he preached, his eyes poured forth plenteous floods of tears, and when he prayed, there was a divine fervor and heavenly prevalence in every petition.

Now so it is with many Christians. They seem to be the very picture of godliness; their life is admirable, and their conversation heavenly, but yet they are always crying, —

> "'Tis a point I long to know,
> Oft it causes anxious thought,
> Do I love the Lord or no?
> Am I his or am I not?

So does it happen, that the best of men will question while the worst of men will presume. Ay, I have seen the men about whose eternal destiny I had serious questioning, whose inconsistencies in life were palpable and glaring, who have prated concerning their sure portion in Israel, and their infallible hope, as though they believed others to be as easily duped as themselves. Now, what reason shall we give for this foolhardiness? Learn it from this illustration: You see a number of men riding along a narrow road upon the edge of the sea. It is a very perilous path, for the way is rugged and a tremendous precipice bounds the pathway on the left. Let but the horse's foot slip once, and they dash downwards to destruction. See how cautiously the riders journey, how carefully the horses place their feet. But do you observe yon rider, at what a rate he dashes along, as if he were riding a steeple-chase with Satan? You hold up your hands in an agony of fear, trembling lest every moment his horse's foot should slip, and he should be dashed down; and you say, why so careless a rider? The man is a blind rider on a blind horse. They cannot see where they are. He thinks he is on a sure road, and therefore it is that he rides so fast. Or to vary the picture; sometimes when persons are asleep, they take to walking and they will climb where others will not think of venturing. Giddy heights that would turn our brain seem safe enough to them. So there be many spiritual sleep-walkers in our midst, who think that they are awake. But they are not. Their very presumption in venturing to the high places of self-confidence, proves that they are somnambulists; not awake, but men who walk and talk in their sleep. It is, then, I say, really a matter of serious questioning with all men who would be right at last, as to whether this child is born to us, and this Son given to us?

I shall now help you to answer the question.

1. If this child who now lies before the eyes of your faith, wrapped in swaddling clothes in Bethlehem's manger, is born to you, my hearer, then you are born again.

For this child is not born to you unless you are born to this child. All who have an interest in Christ are, in the fullness of time, by grace converted, quickened, and renewed. All the redeemed are not yet converted, but they will be. Before the hour of death arrives their nature shall be changed, their sins shall be washed away, they shall pass from death unto life. If any man tells me that Christ is his redeemer, although he has never experienced regeneration, that man utters what he does not know; his religion is vain, and his hope is a delusion. Only men who are born again can claim the babe in Bethlehem as being theirs. "But" saith one, "how am I to know whether I am born again or not?" Answer this question also by another: Has there been a change effected by divine grace within you? Are your loves the very opposite of what they were? Do you now hate the vain things you once admired, and do you seek after that precious pearl which you at one time despised? Is your heart thoroughly renewed in its object? Can you say that the bent of your desire is changed? That your face is Zionward, and your feet set upon the path of grace? That whereas your heart once longed for deep draughts of sin, it now longs to be holy? And whereas you once loved the pleasures of the world, they have now become as draff and dross to you, for you only love the pleasures of heavenly things, and are longing to enjoy more of them on earth, that you may be prepared to enjoy a fullness of them hereafter? Are you renewed within? For mark, my hearer, the new birth does not consist in washing the outside of the cup and platter, but in cleansing the inner man. It is all in vain to put up the stone upon the sepulcher, wash it extremely white, and garnish it with the flowers of the season; the sepulcher itself must be cleansed. The dead man's bones that lie in that charnel-house of the human heart must be cleansed away. Nay, they must be made to live. The heart must no longer be a tomb of death, but a temple of life. Is it so with you, my hearer? For recollect, you may be very different in the outward, but if you are not changed in the inward, this child is not born to you.

But I put another question. Although the main matter of regeneration lies within, yet it manifests itself without. Say, then, has there been a change in you in the exterior? Do you think that others who look at you would be compelled to say, this man is not what he used to be? Do not your companions observe a change? Have they not laughed at you for what they think to be your hypocrisy, your puritanism, your sternness? Do you think now that if an angel should follow you into your secret life, should track you to your closet and see you on your knees, that he would detect something in you which he could never have seen before? For, mark, my dear hearer, there must be a change in the outward life, or else there is no change within. In vain you bring me to the tree, and say that the tree's nature is changed. If I still see it bringing forth wild grapes, it is a wild vine still. And if I mark upon you the apples of Sodom and the grapes of Gomorrah you are still a tree accursed and doomed, notwithstanding all your fancied experience. The proof of the Christian is in the living. To other men, the proof of our conversion is not what you feel, but what you do. To yourself your feelings may be good enough evidence, but to the minister and others who judge of you, the outward walk is the main guide. At the same time, let me observe that a man's outward life may be very much like that of a Christian, and yet there may be no religion in him at all. Have you ever seen two jugglers in the street with swords, pretending to fight with one another? See how they cut, and slash, and hack at one another, till you are half afraid there will soon be murder done. They seem to be so very much in earnest that you are half in the mind to call in the police to part them. See with what violence that one has aimed a terrific blow at the other one's head, which his comrade dexterously warded off by keeping a well-timed guard. Just watch them a minute, and you will see that all these cuts and thrusts come in a prearranged order. There is no heart in the fighting after all. They do not fight so roughly as they would if they were real enemies. So, sometimes I have seen a man pretending to be very angry against sin. But watch him a little while, and you will see it is only a fencer's trick. He does not give his cuts out of order, there is no earnestness in his blows, it is all pretense, it is only mimic stage-play. The fencers, after they have ended their performance, shake hands with one another, and divide the coppers which the gaping throng have given them; and so does this man do, he shakes hands with the devil in private, and the two deceivers share the spoil. The hypocrite and the devil are very good friends after all, and they mutually rejoice over their profits: the devil leering because he has won the soul of the professor, and the hypocrite laughing because he has won his pelf. Take care, then, that your outward life is not a mere stage-play, but that your antagonism to sin is real and intense; and that you strike right and left, as though you meant to slay the monster, and cast its limbs to the winds of heaven.

I will just put another question. If thou hast been born again, there is another matter by which to try thee. Not only is thy inward self altered, and thy outward self too, but the very root and principle of thy life must become totally new. When we are in sin we live to self, but when we are renewed we live to God. While we are unregenerate, our principle is to seek our own pleasure, our own advancement; but that man is not truly born again who does not live with a far different aim from this. Change a man's principles, and you change his feelings, you change his actions. Now, grace changes the principles of man. It lays the axe at the root of the tree. It does not saw away at some big limb it does not try to alter the sap; but it gives a new root, and plants us in fresh sold. The man's inmost self, the deep rocks of his principles upon which the topsoil of his actions rest, the soul of his manhood is thoroughly changed, and he is a new creature in Christ. "But," says one, "I see no reason why I should be born again." Ah, poor creature, it is because thou hast never seen thyself. Didst thou ever see a man in the looking-glass of the Word of God—what a strange monster he is. Do you know, a man by nature has his heart where his feet ought to be:—that is to say, his heart is set upon the earth, whereas he ought to be treading it beneath his feet; and stranger mystery still, his heels are where his heart should be:—that is to say, he is kicking against the God of heaven when he ought to be setting his affections on things above. Man by nature when he sees clearest, only looks down, can only see that which is beneath him, he cannot see the things which are above; and strange to say the sunlight of heaven blinds him; light from heaven he looks not for. He asks for his light in darkness. The earth is to him his heaven, and he sees suns in its muddy pools and stars in its filth. He is, in fact, a man turned upside down. The fall has so ruined our nature, that the most monstrous thing on the face of the earth is a fallen man. The ancients used to paint griffins, gryphons, dragons, chimeras, and all kinds of hideous things; but if a skillful hand could paint man accurately none of us would look at the picture, for it is a sight that none ever saw except the lost in hell; and that is one part of their intolerable pain, that they are compelled always to look upon themselves. Now, then, see you not that ye must be born again, and unless ye are so this child is not born to you.

2. But I go forward. If this child is born to you, you are a child, and the question arises, are you so? Man grows from childhood up to manhood naturally; in grace men grow from manhood down to childhood; and the nearer we come to true childhood, the nearer welcome to the image of Christ. For was not Christ called "a child," even after he had ascended up to heaven? "Thy holy child Jesus." Brethren and sisters, can you say that you have been made into children? Do you take God's Word just as it stands, simply because your heavenly Father says so? Are you content to believe mysteries without demanding to have them explained? Are you ready to sit in the infant class and be a little one? Are you willing to hang upon the breast of the church, and suck in the unadulterated milk of the Word—never questioning for a moment what your divine Lord reveals, but believing it on his own authority, whether it seemed to be above reason, or beneath reason, or even contrary to reason? Now, "except ye be converted and become as little children," this child is not born to you; except like a child you are humble, teachable, obedient, pleased with your Father's will and willing to assign all to him, there is grave matter of question whether this child is born to you. But what a pleasing sight it is to see a man converted and made into a little child. Many times has my heart leaped for joy, when I have seen a giant infidel who used to reason against Christ, who had not a word in his dictionary bad enough for Christ's people come by divine grace to believe the gospel. That man sits down and weeps, feels the full power of salvation and from that time drops all his questionings becomes the very reverse of what he was. He thinks himself meaner than the meanest believer. He is content to do the meanest work for the church of Christ, and takes his station—not with Locke or Newton, as a mighty Christian philosopher—but with Mary as a simple learner, sitting at Jesus' feet, to hear and learn of him. If ye are not children, then this child is not born to you.

3. And now let us take the second sentence and put a question or two upon that. Is this son given to us? I pause a minute to beg your personal attention. I am trying, if I may, so to preach that I may make you all question yourselves. I pray you let not one of you exempt himself from the ordeal but let each one ask himself, if it true that unto me a Son is given? Now, if this Son is given to you, you

are a son yourself. "For unto as many as received him to them gave he power to become the sons of God." "Christ became a Son that in all things he might be made like unto his brethren." The Son of God is not mine to enjoy, to love, to delight in, unless I am a son of God too. Now, my hearer, have you a fear of God before your eyes—a filial fear, a fear which a child has lest it should grieve its parent? Say have you a child's love to God? Do you trust to him as your father, your provider, and your friend? Have you in your breast "The spirit of adoption whereby we cry, Abba, Father?" Are there times with you when on your knees you can say, "My Father and my God." Does the Spirit bear witness with your spirit that you are born of God? And while this witness is born, does your heart fly up to your Father and to your God, in ecstacy of delight to clasp him who long ago hath clasped you in the covenant of his love, in the arms of his effectual grace? Now, mark my hearer, if thou dost not sometimes enjoy the spirit of adoption, if thou art not a son or daughter of Zion, then deceive not thyself, this Son is not given to thee.

4. And, then, to put it in another shape. If unto us a Son is given, then we are given to the Son. Now, what say you to this question also? Are you given up to Christ? Do you feel that you have nothing on earth to live for but to glorify him? Can you say in your heart, "Great God, if I be not deceived I am wholly thine?" Are you ready today to write over again your consecration vow? Canst thou say, "Take me! All that I am and all I have, shall be for ever thine. I would give up all my goods, all my powers, all my time, and all my hours, and thine I would be—wholly thine." "Ye are not your own, ye are bought with a price." And if this Son of God be given to you, you will have consecrated yourself wholly to him; and you will feel that his honor is your life's object, that his glory is the one great desire of your panting spirit. Now is it so, my hearer? Ask thyself the question, I pray thee, and do not deceive thyself in the answer.

I will just repeat the four different proofs again. If unto me a child is born then I have been born again; and, moreover, I am now in consequence of that new birth, a child. If, again, a Son has been given to me, then I am a son; and again I am given to that Son who is given to me. I have tried to put these tests in the way that the text would suggest them. I pray you carry them home with you. If you do not recollect the words, yet do recollect to search

yourselves, and see, my hearers, whether you can say,
"Unto me this Son is given." For, indeed, if Christ is not
my Christ, he is of little worth to me. If I cannot say he
loved me and gave himself for me, of what avail is all the
merit of his righteousness, or all the plenitude of his atonement? Bread in the shop is well enough, but if I am hungry
and cannot get it, I starve although granaries be full. Water in the river is well enough but if I am in a desert and
cannot reach the stream, if I can hear it in the distance and
am yet lying down to die of thirst, the murmuring of the
rill, or the flowing of the river, helps to tantalize me, while
I die in dark despair. Better for you, my hearers to have
perished as Hottentots, to have gone down to your graves
as dwellers in some benighted land, than to live where the
name of Christ is continually hymned and where his glory
is extolled, and yet to go down to your tombs without an
interest in him, unblessed by his gospel, unwashed in his
blood, unclothed of his robe of righteousness. God help
you, that you may be blessed in him, and may sing sweetly
"Unto us a child is born, unto us a Son is given."

II. This brings me to my second head, upon which I
shall be brief. Is it so? If it is so, what then? If it is so, why
am I doubtful today? Why is my spirit questioning? Why
do I not realize the fact? My hearer, if the Son is given to
thee, how is it that thou art this day asking whether thou
art Christ's, or not? Why dost thou not labor to make thy
calling and election sure? Why tarriest thou in the plains
of doubt? Get thee up, get thee up to the high mountains of
confidence, and never rest till thou canst say without a fear
that thou art mistaken, "I know that my Redeemer liveth.
I am persuaded that he is able to keep that which I have
committed to him." I may have a large number of persons
here to whom it is a matter of uncertainty as to whether
Christ is theirs or not. Oh, my dear hearers, rest not content unless you know assuredly that Christ is yours, and
that you are Christ's. Suppose you should see in tomorrow's newspaper, (although, by the way, if you believed
anything you saw there you would probably be mistaken)
but suppose you should see a notification that some rich
man had left you an immense estate. Suppose, as you read
it, you were well aware that the person mentioned was a
relative of yours, and that it was likely to be true. It may
be you have prepared tomorrow for a family meeting,
and you are expecting brother John and sister Mary and
their little ones to dine with you. But I very much question

whether you would not be away from the head of the table
to go and ascertain whether the fact were really so. "Oh,"
you could say, "I am sure I should enjoy my Christmas
dinner all the better if I were quite sure about this matter;"
and all day, if you did not go, you would be on the tip-toe
of expectation; you would be, as it were, sitting upon pins
and needles until you knew whether it were the fact or
not. Now there is a proclamation gone forth today, and it
is a true one, too, that Jesus Christ has come into the world
to save sinners. The question with you is whether he has
saved you, and whether you have an interest in him. I beseech you, give no sleep to your eyes, and no slumber to
your eyelids, till you have read your "title clear to man-
sions in the skies." What, man! shall your eternal destiny
be a matter of uncertainty to you? What, is heaven or hell
involved in this matter, and will you rest until you know
which of these shall be your everlasting portion? Are you
content while it is a question whether God loves you, or
whether he is angry with you? Can you be easy while you
remain in doubt as to whether you are condemned in sin,
or justified by faith which is in Christ Jesus? Get thee up,
man. I beseech thee by the living God, and by thine own
soul's safety, get thee up and read the records. Search and
look, and try and test thyself, to see whether it be so or
not. For if it be so, why should not we know it? If the Son
is given to me, why should not I be sure of it? If the child is
born to me, why should I not know it for a certainty, that
I may even now live in the enjoyment of my privilege—a
privilege, the value of which I shall never know to the full,
till I arrive in glory?

Again, if it be so, another question. Why are we sad?
I am looking upon faces just now that appear the very reverse of gloomy, but mayhap the smile covers an aching
heart. Brother and sister, why are we sad this morning,
if unto us a child is born, if unto us a Son is given? Hark,
hark to the cry! It is "Harvest home! Harvest home!" See
the maidens as they dance, and the young men as they
make merry. And why is this mirth? Because they are
storing the precious fruits of the earth, they are gathering
together unto their barns wheat which will soon be con-
sumed. And what, brothers and sisters have we the bread
which endureth to eternal life and are we unhappy? Does
the worldling rejoice when his corn is increased, and do
we not rejoice when, "Unto us a child is born, and unto us
a Son is given?" Hark, yonder! What means the firing of

the Tower guns? Why all this ringing of bells in the church steeples, as if all London were mad with joy? There is a prince born; therefore there is this salute, and therefore are the bells ringing. Ah, Christians, ring the bells of your hearts, tire the salute of your most joyous songs, "For unto us a child is born, unto us a Son is given." Dance, O my heart, and ring out peals of gladness. Ye drops of blood within my veins dance every one of you. Oh, all my nerves become harp strings, and let gratitude touch you with angelic fingers. And thou, my tongue, shout—shout to his praise who hath said to thee—"Unto thee a child is born, unto thee a Son is given." Wipe that tear away. Come, stop that sighing. Hush yon murmuring. What matters your poverty? "Unto you a child is born." What matters your sickness? "Unto you a Son is given." What matters your sin? For this child shall take the sin away, and this Son shall wash and make you fit for heaven. I say, if it be so,

"Lift up the heart, lift up the voice,
   Rejoice aloud! ye saints rejoice!"

But, once more, if it be so, what then? Why are our hearts so cold? And why is it that we do so little for him who has done so much for us? Jesus, art thou mine? Am I saved? How is it that I love thee so little? Why is it that when I preach I am not more in earnest, and when I pray I am not more intensely fervent? How is it that we give so little to Christ who gave himself for us? How is it that we serve him so sadly who served us so perfectly? He consecrated himself wholly; how is it that our consecration is marred and partial? We are continually sacrificing to self and not to him?

O beloved brethren, yield yourselves up this morning. What have you got in the world? "Oh," saith one, "I have nothing; I am poor and penniless, and all but homeless." Give thyself to Christ. You have heard the story of the pupils to a Greek philosopher. On a certain day it was the custom to give to the philosopher a present. One came and gave him gold. Another could not bring him gold but brought him silver. One brought him a robe, and another some delicacy for food. But one of them came up, and said, "Oh, Solon, I am poor, I have nothing to give to thee, but yet I will give thee something better than all these have given; I give thee myself." Now, if you have gold and silver, if you have aught of this world's goods, give in your measure to Christ; but take care, above all, that you give yourself to him, and let your cry be from this day forth,

"Do not I love thee dearest Lord?
  Oh search my heart and see,
And turn each cursed idol out
  That dares to rival thee.

Do not I love thee from my soul?
  Then let me nothing love:
Dead be my heart to every joy,
  When Jesus cannot move."

III. Well, now I have all but done, but give your solemn, very solemn attention, while I come to my last head:—If it is not so, what then? Dear hearer, I cannot tell where thou art—but wherever thou mayst be in this hall, the eyes of my heart are looking for thee, that when they have seen thee, they may weep over thee. Ah, miserable wretch, without a hope, without Christ, without God. Unto thee there is no Christmas mirth, for thee no child is born; to thee no Son is given. Sad is the story of the poor men and women, who during the week before last fell down dead in our streets through cruel hunger and bitter cold. But far more pitiable is thy lot, far more terrible shall be thy condition in the day when thou shalt cry for a drop of water to cool thy burning tongue, and it shall be denied thee; when thou shalt seek for death, for grim cold death—seek for him as for a friend, and yet thou shalt not find him. For the fire of hell shall not consume thee, nor its terrors devour thee. Thou shalt long to die, yet shalt thou linger in eternal death—dying every hour, yet never receiving the much coveted boon of death. What shall I say to thee this morning? Oh, Master, help me to speak a word in season, now. I beseech thee, my hearer, if Christ is not thine this morning, may God the Spirit help thee to do what I now command thee to do. First of all, confess thy sins; not into my ear, nor into the ear of any living man. Go to thy chamber and confess that thou art vile. Tell him thou art a wretch undone without his sovereign grace. But do not think there is any merit in confession. There is none. All your confession cannot merit forgiveness, though God has promised to pardon the man who confesses his sin and forsakes it. Imagine that some creditor had a debtor who owed him a thousand pounds. He calls upon him and says, "I demand my money." But, says the other, "I owe you nothing." That man will be arrested and thrown into prison. However, his creditor says, "I wish to deal mercifully with you, make a frank confession, and I will forgive you all the debt." "Well," says the man, "I do acknowledge that I owe you two hundred pounds." "No," says he, "that will not do." "Well, sir, I confess I owe you five hundred pounds," and by degrees he comes to confess that he owes the thousand. Is there any merit in that confession? No, but yet you could see that no creditor would think of forgiving a debt which was not acknowledged. It is the least that you can do, to acknowledge your sin; and though there be no merit in the confession, yet true to his promise, God will give you pardon through Christ. That is one piece of advice. I pray you take it. Do not throw it to the winds; do not leave it as soon as you get out of Exeter Hall. Take it with you, and may this day become a confession-day with many of you. But next, when you have made a confession, I beseech you renounce yourself. You have been resting perhaps in some hope that you would make yourself better, and so save yourself. Give up that delusive fancy. You have seen the silk-worm: it will spin, and spin, and spin, and then it will die where it has spun itself a shroud. And your good works are but a spinning for yourself a robe for your dead soul. You can do nothing by your best prayers, your best tears, or your best works, to merit eternal life. Why, the Christian who is converted to God, will tell you that he cannot live a holy life by himself. If the ship in the sea cannot steer itself aright, do you think the wood that lies in the carpenter's yard can put itself together, and make itself into a ship, and then go out to sea and sail to America? Yet, this is just what you imagine. The Christian who is God's workmanship can do nothing, and yet you think you can do something. Now, give up self. God help you to strike a black mark through every idea of what you can do.

Then, lastly, and I pray God help you here my dear hearers, when thou hast confessed thy sin and given up all hope of self-salvation, go to the place where Jesus died in agony. Go then in meditation to Calvary. There he hangs. It is the middle cross of these three. Methinks I see him now. I see his poor face emaciated, and his visage more marred than that of any man. I see the beady drops of blood still standing round his pierced temples—marks of that rugged thorn-crown. Ah, I see his body naked—naked to his shame. We may tell all his bones. See there his hands rent with the rough iron, and his feet torn with the nails. The nails have rent through his flesh. There is now not only the hole through which the nail was driven, but the weight of his body has sunken upon his feet, and see the iron is tearing through his flesh. And now the weight of his body hangs upon his arms, and the nails there are rending through the tender nerves. Hark, earth is startled. He cries, "Eli, Eli, lama sabachthani?" Oh, sinner, was ever shriek like that? God hath forsaken him. His God has ceased to be gracious to him. His soul is exceedingly sorrowful, even unto death. But hark, again, he cries, "I thirst!" Give him water, give him water. Ye holy women let him drink. But no, his murderers torture him. They thrust into his mouth the vinegar mingled with gall—the bitter with the sharp, the vinegar and the gall. At last, hear him, sinner, for here is your hope. I see him bow his awful head. The king of heaven dies. The God who made the earth has become a man, and the man is about to expire. Hear him. He cries, "It is finished!" and he gives up the ghost. The atonement is finished, the price is paid, the bloody ransom counted down, the sacrifice is accepted. "It is finished!" Sinner, believe in Christ. Cast thyself on him. Sink or swim, take him to be thy all in all. Throw now thy trembling arms around that bleeding body. Sit now at the feet of that cross, and feel the dropping of the precious blood. And as you go out each one of you say in your hearts,

> "A guilty, weak, and helpless worm,
>   On Christ's kind arms I fall,
>   He is my strength and righteousness,
>   My Jesus, and my all."

God grant you grace to do so for Jesus Christ's sake. May the grace of our Lord Jesus Christ, and the love of God, and the fellowship of the Holy Ghost, be with you all, for ever and ever. Amen and Amen.

Made in United States
Orlando, FL
14 December 2021

11712983R00075